Dear Zach —
You are the most
adorable guy on
the planet.
Good luck and
breathe!! You are
a superstar.
With love.
challah-lujah

954 907-7327

from **hell**

to **challah**

Praise for *from hell to challah*

"All it took to send Shari Wallack to a mental institution was an alarming cascade of life crises and one very minor worldwide catastrophe. Once sprung, she found herself on a spontaneous cross-country road trip to find peace of mind through food and friendship. Both hilariously raw and unflinchingly honest, her book *from hell to challah* shows how with hope, challah, and help from a handful of red cardinals, she rediscovered her reasons for waking up in the morning. It's a joyful journey worth taking!"

Jon Cryer, Comedian and *Two and a Half Men* Emmy-winning Actor

"Shari Wallack is a wonderful and charming writer with an eye for the details that make life worth living. During this lost year comes a stirring, heartfelt, and funny story of how you can be found. And with her recipes, you're in for some extra treats."

Phil Rosenthal, Creator of *Everybody Loves Raymond* and *Somebody Feed Phil*

"Shari Wallack packs more than a dollop of self discovery and painful truths as she rises from complete despair to a more realized soul. Her harrowing and ultimately redemptive journey about family, faith, and friendship, follows her wrestling with her past and nurturing the good and bad memories to make a more authentic and enlightening future. With honesty, grace, and without shame, Wallack shares a very personal yet universal story about mental health and the power of nourishing yourself."

Kevin McCollum, Four-time Tony award-winning Broadway and Film Producer

"*from hell to challah* is a shocking, funny, and honest diary of a woman who experiences loss and decides to take a road trip during a pandemic. Shari's journal captures her thoughts laid bare as she attempts to escape an examination of herself only to discover that road trips aren't always the dream journeys we imagine them to be. You will howl with laughter and your mouth will fall open more than once at her antics. Through it all, Shari holds nothing back and comes out the other side with a batch of new recipes for life."

David Quinn, Co-founder of Allrecipes.com

"Shari Wallack takes us on an incredible and tantalizing journey. When life threw her an enormous curveball, she overcame, conquered, and found passion again! Shari is certainly an inspiration and a shining star. And her hilarious stories had me in stitches!"

Michelle Fee, CEO of Cruise Planners

"I don't even cook (my favorite kitchen appliance is the fire extinguisher) but I was inspired to bake challah after reading Shari Wallack's hilarious travelogue. She'll take you across the country while progressing through her own psyche. I could not put it down."

Wendy Liebman, Comedian

"Despite experiencing dark days, Shari Wallack found the strength to grab flour, yeast, eggs, and other unique ingredients to bake challah. Each braided Jewish bread lifted her spirit and the spirits of family and friends who enjoyed her hand-iwork. With every challah came a story. When woven together these stories created a poignant tapestry of healing, love, and hope."

Rabbi Andrew Jacobs, Ramat Shalom Synagogue

"Get ready for dose after dose of OMG ingredients throughout this comedic journey of real life experiences. Shari Wallack will make you question what's really important in life and what legacy you will leave behind."

Ken Muskat, EVP & Chief Operating Officer of MSC Cruises

"Bravo to Shari Wallack for her jaw dropping, juicy confessional. Wallack delivers honest and transparent personal stories about anxiety, deep depression, dysfunctional family, and what it's like being the designated crazy. She kicked being mentally ill in the balls and took charge of something that was out of her control. I laughed, bit my nails, cried, and then had an urge to run to the kitchen and braid some bread. If you're looking for the read of one of the craziest years on record, this would be it!"

Sasha Charnin Morrison, Author of *Secrets of Stylists*

"Shari Wallack's insatiable curiosity and big heart have made her a masterful collector of people across the globe. It's no wonder that she was able to convince friends and family to house and bake with her in a pandemic. Her story will inspire you to rediscover your authentic self when you feel as though you have lost everything."

Lisa Brescia, Broadway Actor and Assistant
Professor at Missouri State University

from hell
to challah

rising from fragile to fearless,
one grain at a time

a memoir

shari wallack

RADIUS

Radius Book Group
New York

Radius Book Group
A Division of Diversion Publishing Corp.
New York, NY
www.RadiusBookGroup.com

For more information, email info@radiusbookgroup.com.

First edition: July 2021
Hardcover ISBN: 978-1-63576-912-8
eBook ISBN: 978-1-63576-815-2

Library of Congress Control Number: 2021901840

Manufactured in the United States of America

10 9 8 7 6 5 4 3 2 1

Cover design by Tom Lau
Interior design by Neuwirth & Associates
Illustrations and cover art by Lindsay Rosenthal

for arnon

May your memory be a blessing to all whose lives you touched.
Thank you for sharing your words of encouragement and wisdom with
me. You made me laugh and feel joy with every visit and every bite of your
falafel. You would have understood why I took this soul-bending journey.
Thanks for being with me every step of the way.
The cardinals gave me comfort.

for rachel and jake

Being your mother is the greatest privilege and my favorite title.
Please follow your dreams and be authentic. Find joy. Be grateful.
You are enough! No matter what happens, I will be right here.
And remember, never EVER give up!

Thank you so much for
allowing me to share my
memoir with you.
You are not alone.
Keep moving forward.
It's going to be okay.
One breath.
One day.
One grain at a time.
♡ Shari

table of contents

foreword

by Adam Goldstein

I have known Shari Wallack for more than twenty years as a standout professional in the cruise industry. She and her small but highly capable team of dedicated ladies at Buy the Sea have reached the highest echelon of cruise travel distribution. They specialize in booking corporate and incentive travel for groups, including those large enough to charter their own ships. During my tenure as President and CEO of Royal Caribbean International, I watched Shari and her team receive Account of the Year accolades on an annual basis.

To succeed as an entrepreneur in this business requires a lot of skill, nerve, and relationship building. I think of Shari as equal parts smart, relentless, and hilarious. Her persistence knows no bounds. She can negotiate just about anything. I got to know her on a more personal basis when we both happened to be flying on the same Southwest flight from Baltimore to Fort Lauderdale. I was one of the last to board the flight. Shari discouraged everyone ahead of me from taking the middle seat next to her, saved it for me, and then demanded that I sit in her aisle seat to enjoy the extra legroom. I learned how she became, in her words, an accidental entrepreneur, and what was behind the success of her company—in a word, passion. Passion to sell. Passion to serve. Passion to succeed.

After reading this memoir, it became abundantly clear to me that I knew so little about Shari, much less what she was going through in 2020. I did previously understand she was zany in a comically and proudly New York-Jewish way. When I look back on the texts we exchanged during her travels, I interpreted her angst as normal for the predicament all of us in the cruise industry suddenly found ourselves in. After all, in January 2020, the cruise experience arguably enjoyed the most positive momentum in the entire travel industry, and Shari's business model was completely focused on selling and delivering this experience. So much for focus!

foreword

In hindsight, I completely failed to comprehend the depth of her pain and anxiety or what she felt she needed to do to piece her life back together again. I did not realize COVID-19 had robbed her of her passion and left her in an abyss. With extraordinary determination and a lot of help from her friends, I now understand how Shari recovered the passion that is her rocket fuel and why she is determined to put her renewed passion to use not only for continued business success, but more importantly, for the benefit of the world around her. I applaud her for putting her whole, multifaceted, and endlessly humorous self on display to help all of us navigate our individual journeys through good days and bad.

As one can surmise from this book's title, *from hell to challah,* the loaf of bread traditionally baked to celebrate the Jewish sabbath plays a vital and uplifting role throughout Shari's remarkable progression of experiences during the pandemic. Shari describes how she plaits or braids the strands of a challah before baking it to perfection in a dizzying array of variations. But the challah metaphor runs much deeper than the actual bread with which she charms her way through the kitchens and taste buds of friends and family during her unique three-month American journey. It reflects the unraveling and re-raveling of her mental health, her relationships, her priorities, and her attitude towards the future. Again, I applaud the courage and transparency with which Shari invites us into the destruction and reconstruction of the interwoven strands of her life.

As you devour this engaging memoir, you will vicariously eat more wonderful food than you have ever vicariously eaten before. I actually weighed myself before and after a few of the chapters, just to be sure I wasn't gaining weight from reading about food. You will also consume Shari's attention to detail, love of life, and insight into the diverse characters in her world. After you are sated with this rollicking commentary on the human condition, it will be up to you to determine how to plan for and deal with the meals that life serves up to all of us. *L'chaim!*

prologue

from hell to challah takes place from July 1 to October 9, 2020. It is a physical, emotional, and spiritual memoir. Everything in the book is accurate, although some names have been changed to protect friends, family members, clients, and others.

This personal story transpires during our nation's struggle with coronavirus. It was written to shed light on the state of our mental health system and to offer encouragement to those who suffer from mental illness, anxiety, and depression. It is not a how-to manual, yet it is my hope that others will read it and find their own ways to cope with life's challenges and darkest moments.

from hell to challah chronicles a three-month long road trip beginning with crippling depression and ending in spiritual and emotional emancipation. It will take you from three days in a mental hospital on an adventure of recovery, reflection, and revelation. It is a story of prayer, Jewish food, friends, and even some new business. This is my version of *Eat Pray Love*, COVID edition. It's the time I realized that if I love and care for myself, I can love others in a healthy way, while putting my anxious energy into cooking and freely sharing my time and talents.

I am grateful to have had the financial resources to explore the wonderous United States of America, connect with family and friends, and chronicle this voyage.

May you find peace, comfort, joy, and purpose.

A percentage of the proceeds of this book will be donated to nonprofit organizations that help Black and trans women who struggle with mental illness.

get a journal

When COVID-19 started, I knew it would take its toll on my mental health. I struggle with generalized anxiety disorder, which can (and has) put me into a deeply depressive state. I have taken Zoloft, Paxil, Prozac, and Lexapro to balance my serotonin levels. I relied on Xanax and Ambien to relax me and help me sleep. Many years ago, I was on an oxycodone kick (I was happy to take anyone's leftover surgery meds) to numb the heart-throbbing, head-pounding feeling I get when I am very anxious. When I experience intense anxiety, it feels as if I am completely out of control and spiraling downward. The pills helped, especially the oxy. I could breathe, focus, and get through the day. The problem? You cannot go to Walgreens and get these controlled substances over the counter, and, of course, no one will prescribe opioids for anxiety. I was doomed. I was convinced COVID would be the end of me.

In mid-April 2020, I called my psychiatrist. He has saved me from myself before.

I asked, "Doc, please get me through COVID alive. Put me on the right meds. I am not eating. I have lost fifteen pounds. I have no appetite, and all I do is cry. I cannot sleep. I feel out of control. I need you to fix this."

The doctor put me back on Lexapro and added in Mirtazapine.

He said, "Shari, I promise you, it is going to be okay. Just listen to me and do what I tell you to do."

How could it be okay? It is never going to be okay!

"Oh, and get a journal," he said. "Write in it every day."

A journal? Blech!

"What is the point of a journal?" I asked.

"Well," he said, "You can see how you are feeling today, tomorrow, and weeks from now. You can look back and see how you were doing then, as opposed to today."

Will I really care in September how I felt in March? Isn't this a total waste of time?

I did not feel like writing anything. I just wanted to crawl under the covers and never come out.

Okay, fine! I will get a journal.

Just so happens Carnival Cruise Line had given me a nice leather-bound red one years ago, and I never opened it. No time like the present.

April 15, 2020

I hate my life. I hate everything. Business sucks; it is falling apart all around me. I feel out of control. I feel lost. I do not want to get out of bed. I want to go to sleep and wake up in 2022 or not wake up at all. I feel helpless. The meds are not working. My kids do not want to be around me. My mother does not respect my boundaries. My father is in his own world. I have not been a good mother. I did everything wrong. I am sorry. I just do not know if I have the energy for COVID and what it will take to build back my business—if there even is one left when this is over. I have no purpose if I do not have Buy the Sea. Maybe I have just had enough. I am a failure. I am unhappy. I feel trapped. I want a do-over. It feels like it is never going to get better. This sucks! Good night.

September 15, 2020

I am so very grateful. Life is beautiful. Everything is exciting. I am so lucky to have found passion and purpose on my journey of self-discovery. I have never wanted to travel alone, yet being on the road for the past ten weeks has been so freeing and inspirational. I am excited to wake up and welcome each day. I love what every hour brings, and I have not been bored for a single minute. I have faced my fears and found hope, human connection, joy, and new destinations. This country is filled with amazing sights and wonderful people. I cannot believe that it took a pandemic for me to fly and embrace my inner gypsy.

I have always said that I am followed by a lucky star. Perhaps other people call that G-d. I am blessed and happy. The funny thing is that we still have COVID, political turmoil, and systemic racism that continues to hurt my friends and all people of color. And the travel industry is on life support. I was always told that life is 10 percent what happens to you and 90 percent how you deal with it. Thank you, lucky star, for helping me deal with it. I am happy I stuck around to see how it all unfolded. It has been quite a remarkable journey. Namaste!

WAIT, what? Did the same person write those two journal entries? Impossible, right? How can anyone be depressed and out of control on April 15 and have it so seemingly together on September 15?

fragile

It was the evening of July 1

For several months, I had watched Buy the Sea, my cruise and all-inclusive resort brokerage business, lose two-thirds of its programs and profits for 2020. Every day since March 12 had been full of event cancellations, program rescheduling, and refund demands. Each call was anxiety provoking. My friends were being furloughed and fired throughout the industry daily. LinkedIn and Facebook were exploding with requests for help from colleagues searching for work. Many were abandoning their rentals to live with their aging parents.

I spent my time straddling thoughts that would have seemed unconscionable just a few months prior. Should I reduce salaries or furlough my employees? The PPP loan covered a small amount of our expenses, but only for a short time. I was getting Zoomed out. I could not focus. Going to the office made me sad, mad, lonely, and nervous, although I was blessed with Jaci, Caryn, Sandy, Ana, and Robbyanne, the best team in the industry. 2020 was on target to be our best year ever. We were six kick-ass, smart, driven, and successful ladies. How could this be happening? We had just been recognized as Royal Caribbean Cruise's top incentive account for the EIGHTH time. A few months earlier the honor of DSA Supplier Partner for 2019 had been bestowed upon us. A few larger organizations had offered to purchase our little award-winning enterprise just before COVID hit, and I kept saying, "I am not ready to retire yet."

Now, I could be looking at forced retirement. After all, what company is going to take hundreds of their top salespeople on a cruise ship ever again?

The world watched passengers on those quarantined cruise ships for days and then weeks. The cruise industry was getting hammered. It had become the coronavirus poster child. It did not matter that hundreds of more people were dying in nursing homes and rehab facilities than were falling ill on ships, yet our industry was going to take the hit. The convalescent homes were still in business, but the cruise lines ceased to operate on March 12, and almost all ships are still empty. I knew it would be unlikely that cruising would return until sometime in 2021. Imagine trying to convince a client to take a 125 percent future cruise credit on a $2 million program instead of a full refund. It was nearly impossible. Would the cruise lines go bankrupt? There was no guarantee. What a mess!

Picture my mental state on July 1. My two recent Northwestern college graduates were home and not working. My daughter, Rachel, had become a pro bono BLM activist. My son Jake had just received his BA in radio, TV, film, with minors in drama and psychology. He was set to move to New York City to pursue a life as a television and Broadway actor. The entire industry had shut down. There was no work.

My ex-husband, Michael, was still recovering from a massive heart attack and a quadruple bypass he had in December. He is a diabetic and over sixty-five, therefore making him very susceptible to infection. If the kids wanted to see him, we all had to quarantine or see as few people as possible. I am such a social creature that these parameters put more pressure on me, creating additional stress and heightened anxiety.

My girlfriend, Caryn, was dealing with a horrible mold issue in her house that was all-consuming. Because Caryn also worked at Buy the Sea, she was feeling the pain of program cancellations and clients demanding refunds. I mentioned to her that I was slipping into a depression and wanted to fly away. She asked me how I could leave her in her time of need. I didn't want to disappoint her and knew she wanted my presence and support. I stayed in Plantation, Florida, despite my better judgment.

One of my dearest friends, Arnon, died on April 16 of a massive heart attack, leaving behind his wife Teva and two sons. He was only sixty-seven. I was heartbroken. I spent much of my free time with Teva, her boys Etai and Yoni, and Etai's girlfriend, Alexandra. I would go to their house every morning and sit on the patio watching visits of several bluebirds and one red cardinal. Teva explained that when a red cardinal appears, it is a visitor from heaven. Every day I eagerly awaited the red cardinal. I brought food because Jews just do that. We grieve, we laugh, we eat! I started baking challah for them, cooking "cloud eggs," brisket, and truffled potatoes (Alexandra's favorite). I delivered ice cream, sushi, Persian food, and anything else I could think of to console us. Arnon was a force of nature. What would life look like without him?

When his father died, Etai said, "I don't think I will ever be happy again." I felt his pain. I saw his hurt.

Teva added, "He left me at the worst possible time."

We all, however, knew that Arnon would not have survived COVID. His heart could not have handled it. Now our hearts could not handle it, yet together, through music, *shesh besh* (backgammon), food, swimming, stories about *Aba* (dad in Hebrew), and laughter, we were going to somehow make it through.

I continued to feel lonely and anxious, even with the kids in the house. I needed to cheer up. I wanted companionship, and I thought it would be a good idea to have my mother stay with us for a few weeks. It was a recipe for disaster. I was cooking and cleaning constantly. I have a different idea of clean than does my mother. True, I am a bit anal, but I love a clean-looking and smelling house, especially when I am spending so much time in it.

We had a socially distanced Passover with the Wallack side of the family. It was somewhat chaotic and ended in a fight when Mom insisted upon feeding her dog, Jazzie, from her fork. I repeatedly asked her to stop doing it.

I said, "It is disrespectful. In my house, please honor my wishes."

She said, "I do this in my house. What's the big deal? Why are you so uptight?"

I wanted to explode. It was a holiday dinner, after all. Mom would not let up, so I left the table and went to bed. She also insisted on going to work, and we feared she would bring back COVID. We could not go out to relieve the pressure.

No movies, no shopping, no visits with friends, no travel, NOTHING. The most exciting part of our day was a bubble tea run or an early morning trip to Trader Joe's. The house needed to be cleaned continually. The bathrooms smelled like urine. The dogs needed to be bathed. The kids were feeling the pain of COVID and were helping as much as they could, but I was getting more and more depressed. The cleaning lady quit. I wanted to cry, and I did.

Back to the evening of July 1. I had started to go out to a few restaurants and see select friends—VERY few. The kids said that for them to see their dad, I had to stay in my bedroom when he came over.

Why couldn't they just go to his house?

They were giving me their boundaries—not just for Michael to visit, but for other things. I felt outnumbered. I was tired, empty, overwhelmed, downtrodden, and exhausted. As Rachel communicated a list of her requests, I just sat there and recited a monotone "okay" to whatever she asked.

At one point, Jake got exasperated. I know he was having a rough time. Imagine having a virtual graduation from Northwestern University. Four years of hard work, and a big nothing of a commencement. No immediate plans. His acting showcase in NYC, the culmination of his many semesters of drama training—canceled! I am told that hurt people HURT people. He was hurt. He lashed out at me.

Knowing the history of my brother, Jeffrey, who had removed himself from the family thirty years ago, and the fact that my biggest fear has always been losing one or both of my children, Jake said, "You know, our family has a history of sons not speaking to their mothers."

I was at my breaking point, sad, and overwhelmed. I know now that this was not my kids' intention, but I felt attacked and anxious. I didn't want to melt down in front of them. I excused myself, took my backpack of pills, and locked myself in my room. I took one Ambien and went to sleep. Could tomorrow be any worse?

July 2

I unlocked the door to my bedroom early in the morning, went out to get some water, took a Xanax, and went back to sleep. I did not want to face the day. At 10:30 am., Caryn came to check on me and to tell me that she had been trying to call me. We needed to talk about one of our full-ship charters, set to take place in October in the Caribbean. We had been busy making a case for Celebrity Cruises to move the charter to 2022. Time was of the essence. If the cruise line canceled the October schedule before the client agreed to move the program, we would lose our commission. We could not afford to lose any more money.

We talked about business, and then the conversation led to last night, the kids, Michael, and the overall ambience in my house.

I don't remember exactly what happened, but I said, "I want to die. I have had enough. I can't do this anymore."

She said, "If you say that again, I will have to put you in a mental health facility."

I said, "Fine, put me away somewhere. I cannot take this anymore. I don't want to live."

I was crying hysterically. I was so hurt by the thought of never speaking to Jake again. I completely fell apart. Caryn texted her ex-husband, a Broward County sheriff, to ask him what to do. He said that he would have the Plantation police check in on me. That is far from what happened.

Rachel heard me sobbing and came into my room, trying to console me. I ran to the bathroom and threw up. I was nauseous from all the pills I had been taking on an empty stomach. She sat with me on the floor of my bathroom and told me it would be okay. Within minutes there were several armed Plantation police officers in the bathroom, hovering over me. I was frightened. They asked me what happened, and to verify if I had said I wanted to kill myself.

I said, "Yes, but I just had a panic attack. I did not mean it. I am fine. I just want to go back to bed."

They gave me two choices: go with them willingly to Plantation General Hospital or be taken against my will and be Baker Acted. If you don't know what the Baker Act is, it is a mandatory seventy-two-hour hold at a mental health facility. Once there, a psychiatrist observes you and then releases you if you are not likely to hurt yourself or anyone else. They can hold you longer if you are not mentally well, as you become a ward of the state.

It seemed like an easy choice. I asked if I could have Rachel drive me. I did not want to sit in the back of a police car like a criminal. When we arrived at the hospital, I had to relinquish my backpack and my clothes. I was not allowed to have my cell phone or any other possessions. No Xanax, nothing. I was given a gray hospital gown—gray—the color of someone who has been Baker Acted. I felt as if everyone was staring at me and wondering what was wrong with me. I pulled a sheet over myself so that I could hide the color of shame.

I had done what the police told me. I had come of my own free will! I was told by the police that a psychiatrist would evaluate me, and I should be able to leave in three hours. I sat for about an hour until a medical doctor came to chat with me. He asked if I wanted to hurt myself.

I replied, "No, I want to go home."

"Well, we don't have a psychiatrist here for the rest of the day. You have to stay overnight and see someone in the morning," the doctor told me.

Wait! What? "The policeman said that I would be out of here in three hours!" I shouted through tears.

"The police lie, ma'am. That is what they say to get you to come to the hospital,'" he explained.

That is nuts! And don't you ma'am me.

"Can you call MY psychiatrist?" I asked. "He will tell you I am not crazy and that I am not going to kill myself."

"No, we need to evaluate you before we release you," he explained.

"I need a Xanax. I am going to flip out. Please get me a Xanax!" I screamed.

It took two and a half hours to get ONE Xanax.

Was it flown in from New York?

I asked if I could call my kids. A nurse pointed me to the phone. The kids were relieved to hear from me. I did not realize that they were sitting in my car in the parking lot, worrying. While I was being admitted, they had left and returned with a sandwich, a real blanket, pajamas, a pillow, and two books. I could only wave to them from the window and was reprimanded within minutes to get back into my stretcher, where I sat until 10:30 p.m. that evening, about twelve hours after I arrived. I was getting agitated and asked for another Xanax.

A nurse came over and said, "I have something that will work more quickly for you."

I had gently pulled out my IV. It was the one they inserted earlier to take my blood and make sure I was not a drug addict. The nurse slid a new one into my arm and pumped something delicious into my veins.

"Yum!" I exclaimed. "What is this? I love it!"

"It's a cocktail of Ativan and Benadryl," she replied.

I was feeling no pain. I was floating. This was the best I had felt in months. It was fabulous, like the Versed they give you before surgery. I did not care if they left me on that stretcher forever. I waited to be moved to a room so that I could see the psychiatrist in the morning and go home at last. At midnight, a doctor came to speak with me. I was loopy. He told me that there was no bed for me at Plantation General, and they had to move me to another facility. He gave me three choices: Tamarac, Hollywood, or Aventura.

I commanded, "Whichever gets me in to see a psychiatrist the quickest is where I want to go." He told me that they were all the same, so I chose University Hospital in Tamarac. At 1:00 a.m. on July 3, I was loaded into an ambulance and driven from Plantation to Tamarac.

The next thing I remember was being wheeled down a white hallway and put into a chair. There was no COVID test. I was given a mask. A lady came to speak with me. The room was dark.

"Do you know where you are?" she asked.

I replied, "Tamarac?"

She explained, "You are at University Hospital, the Pavilion."

I was tired and just wanted to go to bed. I would see a doctor and be out of there in the morning. I just wanted to sleep.

I was escorted into a room and given one towel, two microscopic bottles of bodywash, a toothbrush, and toothpaste. There was a young Black girl in the bed next to mine. Both of her feet were bandaged. She was shredding her pillow.

When the nurse came in to talk to her, she uttered, "My name is Jane Doe."

Oh my G-d, I am in the nut house!

July 3

I woke up. Jane Doe was sitting in bed. She had false eyelashes on only one eye, bandaged feet, and a glazed look. I tried to talk to her, but I could see she was not playing with a full deck. I got out of bed and went to the reception desk. "May I please speak with someone? I do not belong here. There has been a mistake. I need to see the psychiatrist so that I can go home."

Out came Maryann, a middle-aged white lady with a kind face and a soft temperament. "Hi, Ms. Wallack. I am Maryann, the nursing supervisor. Can I help you?"

I replied, "Yes. Please call me Shari. I am not crazy. I want to go home."

"Everyone says that," said Maryann. "No one thinks they are crazy. If you try and convince anyone you are NOT crazy, the crazier you sound," she explained. "Please wait here." She pointed to a seat inside the television room in Unit 3, which I came to learn was the geriatric unit. WTF?

I sat down and waited and waited and waited for three hours. Next to me was a lady who was ready to be released. She, too, had told someone she wanted to kill herself, spent three glorious days at the Pavilion, and was supposed to get out that afternoon.

She told me, "Regardless of what you say to the medical staff, you have been Baker Acted, and you will be here for seventy hours. Just get used to it and make the best of it."

Three days? I am going to be putting up with this bullshit for three days? No way! I am going to get out of here. I can negotiate anything. I have privilege and power. I have money and status. I own a business, a house in Plantation, and an apartment in Manhattan. I have two cars. I have a lawyer. I have family. I have friends. Surely, I can get myself out of this shithole.

The psychiatrist assigned to my case, Dr. Watkins, and his stunning assistant, Sierra, came to speak with me. They never asked me what happened.

Watkins stated, "You are here because you said you wanted to kill yourself." He then asked, "Do you want to hurt yourself?"

Without hesitation, I replied, "Absolutely not."

They took some notes and then told me they would see me the next day.

"Wait," I said. "I was told that all I needed to do was meet with you and then I could go home. Can't I go home today?"

"No," Watkins said. "Maybe tomorrow."

UGH. Seriously?

"Why not?" I questioned.

"We need to make sure you are not going to hurt yourself before we let you go," he replied.

I had to find a way to get through the day. I decided to see what was for lunch. There were Styrofoam boxes for everyone. I took one and sat next to a lady in a wheelchair. She was alone. I decided to join her. Having never been inside a mental hospital, I had no idea what to expect. Was everyone a stressed-out mom who had a lapse in judgment? Or could these people be seriously ill? I was going to find out.

I opened the lunch. Fried chicken, potatoes, wilted spinach. I was hungry, and I was going to eat it. I put some ketchup in the container. I picked up my fork and knife and cut a piece of chicken.

In a monotone voice, the lady next to me said, "I am cutting my chicken."

I dipped a piece of chicken into the ketchup.

She said, "Mmm, I love ketchup."

I put the chicken in my mouth.

She said, "Mmm, I love chicken. I am eating my chicken."

Okay, Shari, you are not crazy. THIS is what crazy looks like.

I got up and moved to a table to sit alone. There were elderly men and women roaming the hallways. All had serious mental conditions ranging from schizophrenia to bipolar disorder to everything else you can imagine. Some were drooling. One was scooting and spinning around the hallways in her wheelchair. Another was dancing to music in her own head. It was fucked up!

I asked for Maryann. Does this make me a "white Karen"?

"Maryann," I said. "I cannot handle this. Is every unit like this one? These people are nuts. I cannot do it. Help me. Please."

She said, "Okay, I have a bed in Unit 1. I can move you there."

"What is Unit 1?" I asked.

"It is a higher-functioning unit, and the residents there are much younger," she replied.

"Okay, can I go now?" I demanded gently.

"Yes," she confirmed.

I packed up my blanket, books, and toothbrush, and off I went. It had to be better over there.

I walked into Unit 1 and was greeted by the residents, starting with "Big Six," a Harlem Globetrotter doppelganger. He measured six feet, seven inches and stood there in his Captain America pajamas, glaring at me. He comes in regularly for thirty days at a time to kick a reoccurring drug habit. Then Claire, a bipolar lady in her fifties who walked around with an inside-out blouse and black leggings, telling everyone that she loves coffee and wants to sell life insurance because "everyone knows that bipolar people like life insurance." She frequently broke out into random conversations in French. It was beyond strange. She would tell me on the hour, "I am bipolar. Did I mention that?"

Then there was Ashleigh, who had worked as a barista at Starbucks. She was in for taking three hundred clozapine and trying to kill herself. This was not the first time she had done this. She took the pills and then called the police, hoping to be dead by the time they arrived. Tragic! Nineteen years old. As a child, she had been sexually assaulted by a family member. She had been living with her grandmother, who told her she was fat and ugly and would never amount to anything. I think I would take pills too.

Eighteen-year-old Angela was in for anger issues. There was a twenty-three-year-old Filipino girl who was there for telling her husband that she wanted to slit her wrists. The pair had a two-year-old son. While in the Pavilion, she found out that the husband had filed for divorce. It was not a good scene.

Next up: Samantha, a twenty-one-year-old EMT with a chemical imbalance, and a fifty-year-old gang member whose entire face was tattooed—including his scalp! I could not stop staring. His wife's name, Rachel, was inked into the right side of his face, and the "a" was his eye. Seriously. Frightening! I had nightmares about him.

And finally, there was my roommate, Sally, who was in for medicine rebalancing. It is possible she had an IQ of eighty. She did not understand the rules of Monopoly, so she did not want to play.

I said, "Okay, let's play a different game. Can you play Scrabble?" I asked her.

"I don't know," she replied. "I don't spell very well."

That was an understatement. We played Scrabble with "Anger Girl" and "Big Six," but I had to take my turn and Sally's because she could make only three-letter words. I felt sorry for her.

When we were not playing games, there was a television in the unit, playing cartoons and Disney movies. This was going to be a long day. The only bright light was Samantha, who was sitting by herself doing a puzzle. As I got closer, I could see the pieces coming together. She was completing a puzzle of a red cardinal sitting on a barn.

I asked, "Why the red cardinal?"

She said, "I asked my mom for a scene of a farm, and this was the best she could do."

Arnon! Maybe I was meant to be here. Like the cardinals that visited Teva, this was a sign.

The nurses and aides on the unit were mostly inept. A few were nice and helpful. Arthur and Rosa were lovely. The rest were either unqualified, rude, dismissive, or downright scary.

There was no counseling. No one on staff asked me why I was there. I was given meds in the morning and meds at night. There were no psychologists asking what happened and how they could help. We had thirty minutes of outside time in a fenced-in courtyard, much what you would expect on *Wentworth*. It WAS prison.

I was not allowed to wear a bra because it had an underwire, and I might hurt myself.

WHAT?

I walked around in pajamas unless I wanted to sport that gray gown of shame. Demoralizing.

July 4

Surely this was the day. Watkins and Sierra would come to see that I was fine and discharge me. No such luck.

They approached me as they had the day before and asked the same question: "Do you want to hurt yourself?"

"NO!" I said emphatically.

They looked me over. I smiled to show them I was happy. I was far from happy but was playing the game. They walked away.

I saw Maryann coming in my direction. I asked her, "Can I please go home now?"

She questioned me, "Did you ask Dr. Watkins to go home?"

"No, I didn't ask him. Isn't that implied?" I asked her with tears in my eyes.

"Well, if you didn't ask him specifically to go home and fill out a right-to-release form, you can't leave. It takes twenty-four hours after you fill out that paperwork to go home," she explained.

WHAT? She could not be serious. Not being a part of the frequent guest program at the Pavilion, how in the world could I know that I had to do that?

"Please, Maryann, ask Watkins if I can go home," I begged.

"I will try," she replied. An hour later she came to find me.

"Watkins didn't sign the release, but the Baker Act has been lifted," she told me.

"Lifted? So, I am here of my own free will now? I can go home?"

"No, only Watkins can release you," she said.

"WHAT?" I started to cry. "There is no Baker Act, and I am here of my own free will, but I cannot leave?" I screamed. "That makes no sense!"

"Just fill out the right to release, and if all goes well, you will go home tomorrow," Maryann explained.

Okay, whatever, I could suck it up for one more day. I had already read the two books: *You Are a Badass*—apparently not bad enough—and *The Shoemaker's Wife*. I was bored to tears, but I had to hold it together and get out of there on Sunday. I remember singing the lyrics to Kelly Clarkson's "Stronger."

If it doesn't kill me, will it make me stronger? Do I have enough fight in me to get through this? Yeah, I'm a fighter and always have been. But how do I get there from here? And where exactly is "there?"

The fourth of July was awful. First—COVID. Second—this senseless hospital stay. Wait, maybe not. I got some paper and a pencil—a tiny golf pencil that was barely sharpened—and I started to write. What if I pretended that I was on a site inspection of a lousy hotel? What if I could do a report on this horrible place and get some of the staff removed? What if I could make it better for the next people who unfortunately found themselves in this position? I needed to fill twenty-four hours. I started to write about the parade of ants on my bed and nightstand, about the awful front-desk people and the scary night nurse. That is what I needed to do.

July 5

Sunday morning, I was greeted by Sierra.

"Shari, are you ready to go home?" she asked in a calm, kind voice.

Ready? It had been only seventy-two hours but felt like a lifetime. I had done my time. I was going to get out and make a difference.

"Yes, please," I replied with a huge grin.

"I know you are going to be okay," she told me.

I thanked her and walked outside, where my children were waiting for me. It felt good to get into my car and drive away a free woman.

I got home, put on my business hat, and crafted a letter to the director of the Pavilion. I copied the CEO of University Hospital in Tamarac.

Here are some excerpts from that letter:

Living conditions

My room, 128, did not have hot water. Only room 127 on the floor offered a hot shower. Even the bathroom in the lobby, which had a shower, had the temperature gauge set so that water never got warmer than cool luke. I asked politely if I could shower in room 127.

I was told by Camille, "No, you may not go in any other room."

I asked, "What if the girls in there agree to leave—which they did—for ten minutes? Could I just use the shower?"

"NO! These are the rules," shouted Camille.

I exclaimed, "But surely there is a way to have a hot shower!" I took her into my room to feel the water, which was cold. I asked her, "Would you shower in here?"

She replied enthusiastically, "Absolutely!"

I asked for Marie, the supervisor. She saw exactly what I was talking about and said she would send maintenance. Maintenance never came. I told several of the staff that there were ants in my room, in the bathroom on the floor, running up the wall of the shower, in my bed, and on the nightstand. They told me that I must have brought them there because I had put juice or food in my room. I told them I did not.

"We don't have any spray," one of the staff said with a nasty tone.

No one cared. Basically, I should just suck it up. I am sure you also realize that you do not have any shampoo or hair conditioner available. I was supposed to wash my hair in a cold shower with the tiny bottles of cheap bodywash that are rationed out each day. No hairbrushes, only cheap plastic combs. No blankets, only thin sheets to keep me warm at night.

As for entertainment and diversions, there was not a single book to borrow. There were a handful of games. We had thirty minutes of time outside with some music and lame word-search games that you would give to elementary school kids. Nothing was led. We were told to just play on our own.

Staff

Let me start with the good ones: Lisa, Arthur, Rosa, Maryann, Georgette, Sierra. They were kind and treated me and everyone else with respect and care. I think Margo *wants* to do a good job, but I understand that the position is thankless, and she spends her day administering meds, answering repetitive questions, and dealing with all kinds of personalities. She tries, but told me many times the place is understaffed, and she doesn't have time to give the care she would like to give. I cannot imagine being in her shoes. She did tell me upon my release that I was a troublemaker.

I guess if you keep asking questions and try and make the situation better, you are labeled a troublemaker. I am a business owner. I do not just sit by and let things happen, so if that makes me a troublemaker, so be it. I realize none of the staff want to be questioned about the conditions, but I could not sit by and just let it happen to me.

A few of the staff were downright mean and condescending. Camille treated me like an inmate and not a patient.

When I asked her to get Marie because of the shower issue, she said, "I am not calling a supervisor for you. I am not going to argue with you either."

Tammy scared me. Anytime I asked her how she was, she replied with "blessed and always in favor." She had a weird prison-guard vibe about her, a la *Orange is the New Black*. She was not warm, kind, or caring—just weirdly cold and callous.

Food

Breakfast, lunch, and dinner always arrived cold. French fries were undercooked and mushy. Dinners were measly. An overcooked hamburger for lunch does not constitute a meal. Camille kept the freezer locked so that we could not get ice cream when we wanted it. There was never a banana to eat with cereal in the morning; the only fruit ever available was a whole bruised apple or a tiny, impossible-to-peel orange. No peanut butter, no bread EVER, no options. I wished I could just make myself a PBJ.

We could get thin turkey or ham sandwiches at 9:00 p.m. with nothing but one piece of cold cut and bread. The only snacks were individually wrapped cookies. And the same cookies, the same cereal, every day. I could not even get a tea bag. And I question the overly sweet orange soda served with meals. Was that a healthy option?

Actual Help

If I were put in your care because I was depressed, stressed, having anxiety/panic issues, thoughts of suicide—may I ask where the mental help was? I was just given meds. NO ONE ever talked to me about why I was there and how I could get better. NO ONE. I had to beg to speak to a social worker.

I finally got to spend thirty minutes with Jenny on Saturday afternoon. I was told that was done only because Arthur asked her to do it as a special favor. And all that entailed was my telling her what happened. There was little to no advice or help with coping skills. I was NO better off than when I arrived. My meds were basically the same. It was just a few days without social media, family, friends, and love. I got no counseling, no therapy. NOTHING.

So, what was the point of my unfortunate stay with you? You observed me to see if I was stable and then released me? Our mental health system is a tragedy. I saw a poster attached to one of the doors with a schedule for the day, which included group therapy and other activities that never happened while I was there.

I also do not understand what happened when the Baker Act was lifted a day into my stay. Why was I not allowed to leave at that point? I was told that I did not ask to sign a right-to-release form.

I did not know that I had to do that. There was no guidance. I want to understand this system better. I believe it is broken and not effective for someone in my shoes.

I hope that my feedback can help the next person in my situation manage this better. I look forward to seeing the explanation of benefits from my insurance. I am curious to see what the Pavilion says they provided to me while I was there, to encompass charges of more than $24,000. Let me know when we can set up a time to discuss. Thanks so much.

Within twenty-four hours I got a call from an administrator, asking if I would like to set up a meeting. She apologized for the issues I encountered. I told her that when I felt up to it, I would come back, and I guarantee you, I will.

Feeling the need to make a positive impact, I filled my car with samples of shampoo, conditioner, soap, lotion, and perfume that I had collected while staying at hotels. I added toys, games, books, comfort blankets, hair ties, and anything else I could find that would be of use to someone on the "inside." I drove back to the Pavilion later that day and donated all the items. It felt good to give back and to remind myself that I would not ever wear that gray gown again.

I went to sleep early. I had nightmares of being caged. I felt trapped. I imagined I was drowning. I woke up several times dripping with sweat and fear. For the first time in my life, my freedom had been taken away from me. I had no rights. My white privilege did absolutely nothing for me. Everyone was treated the same way inside the Pavilion.

Oh my G-d! Did I really think that I was entitled to skip the line? Get special treatment? Was I perpetuating systemic racism by believing I was better than anyone else or above the law? Did I think that my white skin was going to be of any use? No! That is not me. Get real, Shari. Wake up! You are no different from anyone else and it's time you remove those rose-colored glasses and take a good hard look around you. You have just gotten a dose of reality. It was a tough lesson to learn. And it was about time.

chapter three

i believe i can fly

When I woke up on Monday, July 6, I thought about my next move.

Should I tell anyone other than immediate family? Pretend it never happened? Did I call my psychiatrist? Did I need help? If I stayed home, would this happen again?

I had a lot of unanswered questions. I needed to make a change. I just did not know what. Mom came over to spend a few hours with me. The kids made me food. I looked at my iPhone.

How did I survive three days without any social media, emails, or text messages?

Wait, maybe social media, emails, and texts were part of my problem, the cause of my anxiety, the reason I was melting down. What would it look like if I could be with people instead of technology?

I was tired of waiting for the phone to ring, hungering for a positive email, sitting on Zoom calls, and texting with my cruise and resort suppliers to share disappointing news.

Get on a plane, Shari. Just do it. Go somewhere. Go anywhere. You know how to travel. You can do it safely. The planes are empty anyway.

The morning of July 7, I phoned my brother Jay.

He and I had spoken each day during my imprisonment, and he said, "I am here for you. Just call."

I asked if it would be okay for me to visit him in New Jersey.

He said, "Sure, come."

I bought a one-way ticket from Fort Lauderdale to Philadelphia because the tristate area was requiring a fourteen-day quarantine. I packed a small teal Kiplinger carry-on and a black laptop backpack that Scenic Cruise Lines had given me on a Rhine cruise in 2019. That bag was the only reminder that I was still a business person. I would be gone for a week to ten days, maximum.

I flew with a mask and a shield. Jay collected me at the airport. We had an opportunity to talk about my ordeal on the hour-long ride to his house. He said I was welcome to stay at his house, or I could go with him and his wife, Linda, to their place in Boston. I decided to sleep on it when the phone rang. It was one of my best childhood friends, Celeste.

Coincidentally, Celeste and her husband, Scott, live in Sharon, outside Boston.

I told her what had happened to me, and she said, "Get to me! I will take a few days off from work."

Great! I would drive with Jay, Linda, and their shih tzu Rexie, to Boston. Celeste met us in the city and took me to her house, a paradise if you like honeybees, garden-fresh tomatoes, and every other imaginable vegetable. Flowers abound in their garden, and they have a lovely porch with rocking chairs.

I spent five days with Celeste and Scott. We did not do much, which is exactly what I needed. I had time to think, relax, breathe, and reflect. I felt better. I slept more soundly. I felt loved. There was no conflict. Each morning, I saw a red cardinal. It made sense. I was where I needed to be.

Celeste had to return to her job as the superintendent of Lowell National and Historical Park, and although I knew I was welcome to stay longer, I decided to leave. But where was I going? New York City! In January, I had purchased an apartment on the Upper West Side. It was waiting to be renovated, yet did have a new queen-sized bed in the master bedroom. Wonderful! I could stay there for a few nights.

I took an Amtrak to Penn Station. There was not a soul in my car, and everything was spotless! It was such a pleasant way to travel. Once out of the station, I stopped at a rapid COVID testing center. Within ten minutes I knew I was still COVID negative. I took the empty, spotless subway up to my apartment. This would be the first time I would sleep in my new place. I did not care that it was a train wreck, a handyman special at best. It was mine! I made plans to see my Upper West Side friends, socially distant, of course. It was awesome. I felt connected. I felt human.

I was keeping up with clients, but I was not focusing on business or the lack thereof. I was connecting in person. It felt good. I ventured out into the streets of the "city that never sleeps." It used to be vibrant and busy but was now eerily tranquil. There were few people out. Many windows had been smashed in from the protests, and dozens of businesses were shuttered for good. Unable to provide inside service, the remaining restaurants created outdoor dining space with tables, chairs, umbrellas, and planter boxes.

With so few cars on the road and little noise, it was quite peaceful to dine al fresco in the Big Apple. The waiters, mostly entertainers who work in restaurants as a side hustle, were providing exceptional service to earn healthy tips. This was now their main gig, with no promise of returning to the stage anytime soon. I decided to meet my friends Roy and Andrea for dinner at Thyme and Tonic on Columbus and 83rd. I ordered a lavender martini concoction and some appetizers. I don't usually say I need a drink, but I needed a drink! The food was delicious. It is a great place for anyone with dietary requirements.

Our waiter was a Broadway costume designer who now had nothing to design. He shared stories of his actor friends who had had to give up their apartments and move home for the first time since college. There was a great deal of pain and uncertainty in New York City, something I had not witnessed since 9/11. This usually animated and bustling city had become eerily quiet and far less crowded.

The following morning, I went for a walk in Central Park. As I entered on 81st Street, I encountered a young lady and her French bulldog. I asked for their names.

"I'm Claire Sheridan, and this is my dog Snoopy."

Snoopy? Did she not know that Snoopy is a beagle? Of course she did not. She was from Ireland.

I asked if I could walk with her. That walk turned into a wonderful two-hour chat and a quick friendship. She told me about how frustrating it was to date men in New York, that she had been a lawyer in Ireland but now could work only as a paralegal in the US.

She lamented about her awful landlady. I loved her spirit, charm, and warm personality. I told her that I was on a mission to say hello to everyone I encountered in the park that day. My first hello was to a Black male couple. They were well-dressed and very good-looking. They said hello back and then walked over to us.

"No one ever says hello to us in the park," they said.

Wow! That is crazy. I was drawn to them.

I asked, "What do you both do when you are not walking and talking to strangers?"

One was an investment banker, and the other a cancer surgeon. I was thrilled to meet educated, successful men of color. Never judge a book by its color. I asked if we could be Facebook friends. They obliged. Later that afternoon, there was a FB message waiting for me from these gentlemen. It read, "You were the highlight of our day. Thank you for stopping to say hello."

I was so happy. I had made a difference. As Claire and I continued our walk, we encountered a masked Asian lady walking two very sweet dogs.

Again, I said, "Hello."

She said, "Hi."

I asked about the dogs. They were so interesting looking with piercing blue eyes. I had to know the breed. They were long-haired Chihuahuas. She told us that she was fostering the dogs for a colleague who had been detained overseas. She asked if we knew anyone who would want to take the dogs for a bit because she had to return to work and could not care for them.

"What kind of work do you do?" I wondered.

"I am an anchor at ABC News," she replied.

Seriously?

"I have a close friend who is a reporter for NBC. I randomly met him sixteen years ago on an airplane," I told her.

"Who is your friend?" she inquired.

"His name is Kerry. Kerry Sanders. Do you know him?" I asked.

"Yes, of course," she said. "He used to work for my husband, Neal. Please tell him Ju Ju Chang says hello."

"Okay, I will do that!" I had no idea who she was, but I had to google her when I got home. So, Ju Ju Chang married Neal Shapiro. She converted to Judaism.

Her married name is Ju Ju Shapiro. Jew Jew Shapiro? How fitting!

I felt compelled to tell Ju Ju the details of that first meeting with Kerry:

So, I was sitting in first class on a Delta Airlines flight from Atlanta to Fort Lauderdale in November 2003. I was returning from a conference in Hawaii on a red-eye connection. While on the phone with Caryn, I recounted how random strangers kept commenting on a white gold and diamond Penny Preville necklace I had bought myself for my fortieth birthday a few weeks earlier. I hung up the phone. The stranger next to me said, "Nice necklace."

I replied, "Well, that was original."

He asked, "So, where are you coming from?"

I said, "Hawaii."

He asked why I was there, what I did for a living, where I lived, where I grew up. I was overtired, and not particularly interested in engaging with him. But he seemed nice enough, and he had these electric blue eyes. I asked him, "What do YOU do for a living?"

"I am a correspondent," he replied.

Correspondent? Was that code for spy? What the hell is a correspondent?

"I am a news reporter," he explained.

"A news reporter, like on television? Do I know you?" I asked.

"I don't know. Do you watch the *Today Show*?" he inquired.

"*The Today Show*? THE *Today Show*? Not only do I watch it. I watch it every single morning. When I started working for myself out of my house, I felt lonely. I needed company. and the people on the show make me feel less alone," I explained. "Are you ON the *Today Show*? What is your name?"

"Kerry," he said.

"Kerry? Like Kerry Sanders?" I asked him.

"I am Kerry Sanders," he told me.

"Is THAT what you look like? I only hear the voices in the background while I am working. I don't actually know what any of the reporters look like," I explained.

Kerry laughed. I smiled. Now I was thinking that I was sitting next to a celebrity.

Don't say anything stupid, Shari. Do NOT embarrass yourself with some dumb question or fun fact or whatever else you do when you meet someone famous, get nervous, and completely regret whatever came out of your mouth later. Stay calm. Don't let him think you are the least bit impressed.

And then, I looked deep into his eyes and said the following. On an airplane. "Oh my G-d, you can fulfill my greatest fantasy!"

Kerry's face turned bright red, which made his spectacular azure eyes pop.

"What is your greatest fantasy?" he asked me with trepidation.

"I really want to meet Katie Couric!" I said.

I don't know what he thought I was going to say, but I guarantee you, THAT was not it. His face returned to a pale shade of white. He laughed. I think he was relieved.

"I can make that happen," he told me.

"You can? Really?" I replied.

"Yes, here is my phone number. Let me know when you are back in New York, and I will arrange it," he said.

WHAT? I now had the phone number of a famous reporter? Someone who breathed the same air as Katie Couric? And I was going to meet her someday? Score! Just DO NOT stalk him.

A year went by before I was able to get up to New York, and just as he promised, Kerry set up my meeting with Katie Couric. I was invited into the green room. I met Matt, Ann, and Al. It was a dream come true. Ann Curry let me sit in her news chair to watch Neil Diamond perform. THE Neil Diamond! I could not believe it was really happening. And better yet, I was going to meet Katie.

The production manager told me to sit and wait and that she would bring Katie to me. I waited and waited and waited until I was told that Katie had left the building.

WHAT? Didn't she know she was going to meet Shari Wallack? No!

"I know you came from Florida to meet Katie. Wait here, and I will go outside and get her for you," the production manager told me.

You are going to go and get Katie after she already checked out? For me? Oh my goodness!

And sure enough, Katie came back in the studio to meet me, friend of Kerry Sanders. She introduced herself, and I started to cry. I couldn't help it.

"Are you okay?" Katie asked me.

"Yes, I am just so overwhelmed," I told her.

"Why? And do you want to take some photos with me?" she asked.

"I didn't bring a camera," I told her.

These were the days before iPhones. I explained to Katie that she, Matt, Ann, and Al had become my work family, and they helped me get out of bed in the morning. They kept me company as I transitioned from working for a corporation in an office to working for myself out of my house. I told her I just wanted to meet her to thank her for being there for me.

"So, you don't want a photo?" she asked.

"Well, I guess I do, but I didn't want to seem like a weird fan," I told her.

"Please come back tomorrow as my guest. Ricky Martin is performing. And go get a disposable camera. Let's take pictures," she insisted.

Her guest? Katie's guest? I was going to be Katie Couric's guest the next day? Pinch me. Just don't wake me up from this sweet dream.

I got one of those cheesy cheap disposable cameras at Duane Reade that afternoon. I went back to 30 Rock at six the following morning. I was so close to Ricky Martin while he sang on the plaza that I could see him sweat. Katie introduced him to me. Katie remembered my name! It was amazing.

As for Kerry and me, we have been close friends ever since. I am eternally grateful. And it all started with a necklace that I still wear almost every day.

Back to the story. I left New York City on the morning of July 16 to meet my brother Jay on Long Island. We decided to visit our eighty-nine-year-old father, who lives in Massapequa with his second wife, Lillian. As I raced through Penn Station to catch the train to Long Island, there in front of me was a vendor selling cards. All were lying down on the table, except for one, which was prominently displayed. The one with the red cardinal. I bought it and dashed for the train. I wrote in the card.

Dear Teva, I know it is going to be okay. YOU will be okay. I want you to know that I think of Arnon every single day. I believe he is following me on the journey. That makes me happy. Love, Shari

Jay and I met at the Massapequa Park train station and drove to Dad's house. We enjoyed a Chinese food lunch and some light conversation with Dad and Lillian before Jay drove me to Newark Airport. There, I picked up a rental car and headed to visit my friend Sydney and her family. They had just purchased a small cabin on Swartswood Lake in Northern New Jersey.

I am not much of a camper, and this place is one small step above camping. The bathroom has a compost toilet, which is slightly better than what you find in an outhouse; the shower is tiny, and I think the entire place is seven hundred and fifty square feet, including two bedrooms and a living room/kitchen combo. It was filled with a whole lot of love and acceptance, however.

I adore this family. They are kind, caring, and welcoming. Even though their entire deck had been wiped out by a recent lightning storm and they were somewhat stressed out, they were happy to have me. I bought lots of food and started to cook for them. I was finding joy in the kitchen. It made me forget my troubles. It helped me stay in the moment. If I could do this for Sydney and her family, perhaps I could do this for others.

Could that be the key to getting rid of my anxiety? Was it that simple?

After five days of food, lakeside fun, lots of fattening ice cream, and other naughty desserts, it was time to move on. I drove to the Jersey shore and spent a few nights with the "blue family." I had met the Rosenblum clan on a Mekong River cruise a few years earlier during the Christmas/New Year's break. Each excursion group had a color. Our color was blue, hence "blue family." They were extremely COVID-cautious, so I never went inside the main house. I did not care. I was able to sit on the dock and soak in the sun and crisp ocean air. I had my own room on the first floor, complete with blow-up mattress, bathroom, and washer/dryer. The best part was the amazing outdoor shower.

I went shopping for ice cream, liquor, and other goodies to thank the Rosenblums for their hospitality. While the family went on a private boat trip, I drove back to my brother's place in Manalapan while deciding what to do next. Should I go home? No. I was not ready. If I stayed on the road, where could I go and whom could I see? Would anyone else want a visitor during COVID? How about my cousins in North Carolina? I had been meaning to see them. It had been three years, and I missed the kids.

chapter four

i thank g-d for this day

My first cousin, Casey, is twenty years younger than I am. His father, Norman, is my mother's younger brother. I adore Casey. He is sweet, kind, smart, thoughtful, and caring. He married Melissa, who is an observant Christian. They have four children and a baby girl on the way. Leah (ten), Logan (eight), Livvy (six), and Luke (three) are expecting a special delivery in February.

Casey jokes, "We should call the baby Noelle (no 'L')." The kids cannot quite figure out how I, at fifty-six years old, could possibly be their cousin. So, they call me Aunt Cousin Shari. I love it, so I do not correct them.

On July 23, I called Casey. "May I come and visit, please?" I inquired.

"We would love that! When can you be here?" he asked.

"How do you feel about tomorrow?" I quipped.

"Come on down. Fly to Charlotte, and I will come get you!"

Carry-on bag and backpack in hand, I flew to North Carolina and met Casey at the airport.

"Can you take me food shopping?" I asked.

"Sure," he replied.

Melissa, a certified teacher, homeschools the kids. She was a freshman at Columbine High School when the shooting took place and still suffers from residual trauma. When her children were born, she vowed to teach them herself. Because of this, they are extraordinarily educated, verbal, and bright. Casey works in event production, and with no work in sight because of COVID, I knew they could use some help.

I was thrilled to buy a cartload of groceries and help in the kitchen. It must get tiresome cooking each day for a family of six, so I volunteered to make some meals. The kids were excellent helpers, and together we started to make banana bread, brisket, chicken soup, Bolognese sauce, salads, and finally, challah. The kids had never eaten challah. I decided to make it fun for them and color their first bread all sorts of vibrant shades. I called it acceptance bread as it looked like a rainbow flag. I left out the salt on the first try, and it tasted like Play-Doh.

Leah, who praised everything I made, said, "This is really disgusting."

It WAS really disgusting. Once I got it right, the kids and I decided to add in fun ingredients, and the Almond Joy challah was born. I mixed in chocolate chips, coconut, slivered almonds, crushed graham crackers, and Oreo cookie crumble. Then I tried cinnamon, raisins, and brown sugar, which was Melissa's favorite. Delicious! It was fun. And I was having a "challah-vah" time! The more I kneaded and braided the dough, the less anxiety I felt. Maybe I was on to something? I didn't want to make "angry" bread! Perhaps this was healing-energy challah?

Every night before dinner, my cousins held hands and the kids sang a variation of a *Veggie Tales* song, thanking G-d for the day, the sun, the sky, their mom and dad, and the love that they shared as a family. They included me in their prayers too.

I started to sing with them. It made me feel good to thank G-d. It made me feel grateful to be with this amazing family. MY family. The kids argued over who was going to nap with me, sleep with me, and cuddle with me. I cooked for them, sang with them, cuddled with them, played with them, and showered with them. It was wonderful! I decided I would rent a house in Pidgeon Forge, TN, and we would go for a short family vacation. After all, they had not left the house since March. No restaurants, no playdates, nothing!

We rented a house via VRBO in Pigeon Forge. The owner, Loretta Kilos, seemed like a kind, normal Southern lady during the booking process. Because the rental was so close in, she gave me a $500 discount to make the home more appealing. I could not figure out why she refused to provide access to the washer/dryer. I asked, but she repeatedly said no. Perhaps we could live without one. It's just that we were coming in one Toyota Sienna van with three adults, four kids, and luggage. We did have a roof rack, but even so, we were traveling with suitcases, a cooler, and other supplies. It was tight. We would just have to wear a few things twice.

We arrived at the house, but the cleaning crew had not programmed in our code for the door. I called Loretta, and she sent them over. No problem. I also mentioned that we needed extra bath towels. The cleaners dropped them off.

We immediately named the house the Bear House because everything was decked out in a bear theme: the bedding, the lamps, the dishes, the door, the furniture, the stuffed animals all over the house, everything. Bears galore. It was cute but overkill.

There was not a manual inside the house to tell us where things were. We did not know if there was firewood for the outdoor firepit. We did not know where specific items were located. We had to hunt around. Again, no big deal. I found that the measuring spoons were missing the tablespoons. There was only ONE dish towel. There was no charcoal for the outdoor grill. There wasn't any Wi-Fi—it stated that there wasn't any in the listing, but I had forgotten.

There were no dressers in the bedrooms—only flimsy drawers in the closets. The wood "caps" at the top of the stairs on the banister were not secure. I almost fell when I grabbed one on my way up.

When we first arrived, the televisions didn't work. Loretta had mentioned that we did not need to bring soap for the shower, but there was not any. There were no sponges, just one small Brillo pad to wash dishes. The garbage drawer was on the other side of the kitchen, and there was no disposal in the sink, which made it inconvenient to throw out food bits after rinsing the dishes.

The ice maker did not work, so we had to buy ice. I also told her that the steps at the bottom of the hot tub were wobbly, and one of the kids almost fell upon exiting.

Nothing monumental, but I sent a text to Loretta outlining these items. She did not reply. I was not upset. I just wanted her to know.

When our four days came to an end, we packed up. Casey dropped me off at Knoxville Airport so that I could pick up a car to drive to Memphis, my next stop.

About an hour into the drive, VRBO sent me an email asking me to review the property.

I gave it five stars, the maximum that I could. Despite the items above, we loved the house and had had a great time. Then there was a text box to list anything we thought the next guest should know before staying at the property. I cut and pasted my text to Loretta into that box. It made sense for me to share my experience and offer some tips. I added that we had no comfortable outside seating, that everything was either hardwood or wrought iron. I mentioned that a hammock would have been great. Within minutes, I got the following text:

Loretta: Was there an issue at the cabin for the sheets in the master bedroom to be ripped? Also, we are missing the top sheet on the king bed on the main floor.

Wait! That was the room I stayed in. I did not take her king sheet. I do not even remember there being a top sheet on the bed. Weird.

I called her and then conferenced in Casey. While the three of us were on the phone, I asked Casey about his sheets.

Casey: The sheet was not ripped on our bed.

Me: And I didn't take anything off of my bed downstairs.

Loretta: Okay. Can you tell me why the booster seats were so disgusting?

I told her that we had used them only one time. I did not know how they could have been disgusting. They looked the way they had looked when we took them out of the closet.

The call ended, and I received this text message:

Loretta: And your cousins came later? I meant to ask, how many adults and children did you have?

Me: Huh? We arrived together. Three adults and four kids.

Loretta: Two vehicles.

Why was she even asking this?

Me: No, one. Why?

Loretta: Two vehicles. You are a very dishonest person. You must be a miserable lady. You lied about so many things. We gave you three dish towels for four nights. The cleaning lady brought you more towels for four days/three adults/four children. You should read the VRBO website. No Wi-Fi, but you are too busy running your mouth about the washer/dryer and measuring spoons.

There are dressers with drawers in every bedroom! And there is a truckload of firewood! Are you so miserable that you want to ruin everyone's day? Get a life! Please don't ever inquire about my properties again!

WHAT???? I almost spit out my coffee.

Me: What? We had one car. What are you talking about? I gave you a five-star rating. I do not lie. I did not realize that the firewood was for us. You never answered my text.

Loretta: You called your cousin in another vehicle and did a three-way on our call this morning. You all are liars and crazy people. When you arrived with two adults and three kids in that minivan, you said you had no room for clothes, so you needed a washer and dryer to do laundry.

TWO adults and THREE kids? Not sure where she got her new numbers from.

Me: Yes, at the time of that call, we WERE in two vehicles. My cousin dropped me in Knoxville to pick up my rental car.

Loretta: LMAO . . . you are an amazing liar.

So, I took a photo of the rental agreement and texted it to her. Not sure why I was even engaging, but it had become a game at this point, and I wanted my $400 security deposit.

Me: We wanted a washer/dryer because we had almost no room for the clothes in the minivan. Please do not call me a liar. That is not very nice.

My attempted negotiation with a terrorist?

Loretta: Please leave me alone. I am happy that you are out of my house. I am a blessed lady and do not need your shit. Safe travels.

Me: That's great. Let me know when my $400 security deposit will be returned. Thanks, and have a blessed day.

Loretta: As soon as we get the nasty house cleaned up and the damage assessed. Seven days from today.

Me: Nasty house and damage? Oh my G-d!

Loretta: Did you even get to enjoy the awesome property? You were writing text messages about the measuring spoons two days into the stay. I guess it is hard to sleep when you make up such lies to tell. Dressers! Soap! Firewood! Outside furniture!

Me: Okay, so I really don't get it. Did you READ my review? Did you see the five-star rating? Isn't the purpose of a review to help the next people bring what they need to make their stay enjoyable? I cannot engage anymore. We loved the house. I thought I made that clear in my review. I do not know what you think I am lying about. You refuse to believe that we came in one car after seeing my rental agreement. I do not know what else to say. I wish you a beautiful day.

Loretta: I do not care how many cars you drove. I was just trying to make a point about the truth of all that you say. Why would you say all of the lies?

Maybe the dresser drawers were not big enough for you? You should have asked about the firewood since you asked about everything else. Why would you lie and just keep lying? You are a liar! There are dressers, firewood, and much more.

You sounded like you had a miserable time. You needed sponges, measuring spoons, Brillo pads, ice, a hammock, soft seats, dressers, garbage disposal, new steps for the hot tub, a better view, and charcoal. And a washer/ dryer!

I stopped replying. I just could not reason with a lunatic. I imagine she was looking for a way to keep my security deposit. We were respectful and well-mannered guests. We left the house tidy and did not damage a thing.

Six days later, on August 12, I sent a text:

Me: Dear Loretta, I hope you are doing well. Is there anything I need to do to receive my security deposit tomorrow? Please advise, and thanks so much!

Loretta: Not a thing. If you do not get notification by tomorrow, contact VRBO.

Me: VRBO told me that because I paid the $400 directly to you and not to them, you would be the one to refund the money. If that is not the correct information, please let me know. Thanks so much!

Loretta: You need to wait until the fourteenth before you start complaining!

So, I waited and waited and waited. No refund. Ultimately, I got a final bill. Loretta had changed the amount of the rental and was going to give me back only $83. I called American Express and VRBO and told them it was completely unacceptable. I am still waiting for one or both to rectify this.

I also found out that Loretta gave me a one-star rating as a VRBO guest, warning people to never rent to me. Before COVID, something like this would have upset me. I would have spent far too much time feeling bad and wondering what I could have done differently. Months ago, I might have overreacted and reported this woman to VRBO for her nasty tone and lack of professionalism. So why was I behaving out of character? Why didn't I verbally attack her or tarnish her VRBO reputation? I remember something my friend Sue Hershkowitz-Coore taught me. She said, "Never take away someone's dignity."

It's a good rule to follow. I wasn't going to let Loretta get under my skin. I would take the high road, and as Pumba says in *The Lion King*, I would leave the past in my behind.

I had rented homes with Airbnb and VRBO in the past. This was the first time I had had an issue unless you count that trip to St. Louis in August of 2014. I had rented a van to move Jake into Washington University's dorms. The vehicle was parked in the garage of the house we found on Airbnb. Someone broke into the locked garage and stole everything we spent two full days purchasing. Good times.

As for the Smoky Mountains, I think one trip in a lifetime to Pigeon Forge is plenty. And no, we didn't go to Dollywood. The town is pretty cheesy, like 1970s Orlando before the Disney boom. I was not surprised by the number of pancake houses and ice-cream shops. There was not a gourmet restaurant to be found. Everything was pretty much fast food or corporate chain. I ate quite a bit of tube steaks, salad, and PBJ on challah.

One of the best things that came out of this trip was my cousins' decision to buy a truck and a fifth wheel and drive around the country from September to January, schooling the kids on the road. They are currently in Maine, and I am so excited for them! What a fantastic opportunity for them to go exploring. We plan to meet before the end of the year. I thank G-d for this day.

chapter five

and i'm walking in memphis

People ask me, "What is the best sale you ever made?" I do not know which was the best, but for sure, a highlight of my career has been working with FedEx. I have had the pleasure of partnering with them a few times, procuring full-ship charters on Regent Seven Seas Cruises. I was the first person to be able to convince them to put their President's Club program on a ship, and only because my primary contact, Bobbi Landreth, was a cruise enthusiast. She had been eager to take the program out to sea for years.

Bobbi, her husband Mike, and I had become great friends. They had just built a new house outside Memphis, and until now, I had not had the chance to see it, nor was I able to visit their lake house or take a ride on their boat. Going to Memphis would give me the chance to visit with Natasha, Donna, and Eric, who currently head up the events team at FedEx.

I told Natasha that I wanted to take them someplace special for lunch, but much to my dismay, they picked barbecue.

I HATE barbecue. I think it's disgusting.

Donna ordered fried baloney. It was so awful that it couldn't be spelled *bologna*. I had the turkey sandwich. How bad could that be? Do not ask. I did not think it was possible to ruin turkey breast. I was mistaken.

Bobbi and Mike's new home in Piperton is large, lovely, and perfect, except for the spotty internet. She told me that the development she lives in is trying to get better service, so far to no avail. Bobbi is gluten-free, so no challah on this visit, but I was determined to cook for her all week. Mike was losing weight on Nutrisystem, so it was just us girls. I made mussels Provençal—one of my specialties—rack of lamb, steak, and lots of delicious salads.

When I was in France for vacation several years ago, I ordered mussels from a local seaside café. They were the best mussels I had ever eaten. I asked the waitress to ask the chef if I could come into the kitchen and have him teach me how to make them. I have been serving these to my friends and family for years. Caryn says that I have ruined her for ordering mussels ever again in a restaurant.

mussels provençal

2 bags of mussels, small to medium-sized works best

1 tbsp crème fraiche

1 tbsp unsalted butter

1 cup chopped tomatoes

1 cup chopped onion

¼ cup olive oil

minced garlic—as much as you want

In a heavy stockpot, heat the olive oil.

Add in minced garlic. Once you can smell the garlic cooking, add in the onions and tomatoes. Cook until the onion is translucent. Add in butter and crème fraiche. Stir until dissolved. Add mussels and cover. Lower the heat and cook until the mussels open—about five minutes.

Dinner was served. Bobbi even drank the broth! Score! Fabulous cuisine, a bottle of awesome cabernet, and a good friend can get many people through trauma. We spent hours cooking, discussing religion, and debating politics. I do not usually engage in deep conversations about my political views with clients, but Bobbi was no longer a client, and I figured our friendship could handle it. We agreed that our country was experiencing political turmoil, and we both expressed unease about the upcoming election. I understood that there were conservatives who enjoyed the tax break, supported the crackdown on immigration, and felt that standing up to China and North Korea have benefits. I got that we needed a change in our government. I wasn't convinced we were headed in the right direction.

We bantered back and forth, and during our fireside chats I found that neither of us was extremely left or right. We had more in common than we thought. As we were having breakfast one morning, Biden announced that Harris would be his running mate. I did a pajama-clad happy dance in the kitchen to see a woman on the presidential ticket for the first time. The race had just gotten a little more interesting.

As I exited the kitchen to get dressed, I heard Bobbi say, "Go away already."

I thought she was talking to me. I asked, "What?"

She replied, "Oh, that pesky bird has been coming here every morning. He is a nuisance."

"Where? What bird?" I asked.

"That one. The red cardinal. He is here every morning, tapping on my kitchen window. He drives me crazy," she explained.

"He is not a pest! That is my friend, Arnon!"

She looked at me as if I were nuts.

"Don't chase him away! I want a photo," I said. And in a second, he was gone. I sighed.

"Not to worry," reassured Bobbi. "He will be back in the afternoon on the other side of the house."

And he was. I was somehow in the right place again. Bobbi and I drove about ninety minutes to a town called Counce, where Tennessee meets Mississippi, near Pickwick Dam. There sits their lovely lake house. A few miles down the road is Aqua Yachts Marina, where they keep their boat, *Spontaneity*. The name fit my road trip.

Mike retired from FedEx seven years ago. He is seventy. Bobbi is forty-eight. It works well despite the age difference. They are a wonderful couple, and their form of love includes lots of friendly bickering, culminating in Bobbi getting her way. She is an extroverted extrovert who needs little downtime. She loves to be around people and enjoys talking about just about anything. What I appreciate most is her intellect. She reads and has her facts straight. I thought I was the most extroverted extrovert on the planet, but I do not hold a candle to Bobbi. She can outlast me!

The lake house was lovely. I felt at peace on *Spontaneity*. My days on the boat brought me comfort. I started to forget about my anxiety. I decided I was ready for a phone call with my psychologist, Helene. She has counseled me through the years and has seen me at my worst. Several years ago, when I was extraordinarily depressed, I sat on her couch and asked her, "How long will it take for me to die if I starve myself?"

She said, "You don't want to do that. It is a very long, painful death."

She encouraged me back then to journal, meditate, and take meds. Eventually, I pulled myself out of it, and she was a big part of my recovery. I remember being so miserable that I could not even focus to write in a journal. I am glad that I have somewhat embraced the practice today, although I still do not love doing it.

I told Helene about the stint in the mental hospital, the issues with my kids, the ex-husband, the business, and everything else that had happened since we last spoke. I told her that I was feeling better because I had left town and could be with people again. I shared my cooking and baking adventures. I saw myself on the iPhone screen and could see that I was smiling. I looked lighter. After all the cooking and eating, I had put back on the weight I had lost in March, April, May, and June, but I FELT lighter.

For the first time, Helene said, "I am so proud of you!"

I have never had a therapist say that to me.

She continued, "You have come such a long way. Keep doing it! It suits you."

Therapy is nothing new to me. Therapy was something I generally dreaded, but Helene was different. She was the first psychologist who made me feel good about myself. She was nothing like Mrs. W., the club-footed diminutive social worker whom my mother dragged me to see when I was nine. She always wore black clothing and had pungent body odor. She reminded me of Margaret Hamilton in the *Wizard of Oz*. She was scary. I hated every second.

Mrs. W.: "Shari, do you know why you are here?"

Me: "Because I don't have any friends?"

Mrs. W.: "Because you don't get along with your brother Jay. Your mom said you pulled his hair and dragged him down the stairs. Is that true?"

Me: "He started it."

Mrs. W.: "Shari, you have to learn to get along with people. Do you love Jay?"

Me: "Yes, but he teases me all the time."

Mrs. W.: "Maybe he loves you so much that he just wants your attention. I have a question for you. Think about it. Don't answer right away. If you could take one person with you on a trip, who would it be?"

Me: "Aunt Louise."

Mrs. W.: "You wouldn't take your mom or your dad?"

Me: "No, they don't love me as much as Aunt Louise does. And besides, my parents have to stay home to take care of my brothers."

Mrs. W.; "Are you jealous of your brothers?"

Me: "I don't know."

Aunt Louise is my father's younger sister. She never had kids but always wanted them. In retrospect, it is a good thing she didn't have any. My parents were happy to lend me to Louise on weekends. Mom and Dad had two other kids and wouldn't even notice that I was gone. Louise would take me to her apartment on the Upper East Side of Manhattan and we would have sleepovers. She in her bedroom, and I on the pull-out sofa in the living room. She wouldn't let me sleep next to her because I breathed heavily and it would wake her.

I never told my parents what it was really like staying with her. I didn't want to upset them, and I truly believed that Louise loved me. She used to call me her F-A-V, short for favorite. She would show me her jewelry and tell me that when she died it would all be mine. I never cared about the jewels, which I later found out were mostly gifts from the married men with whom she had affairs. I recall a story when one of her lovers, Seymour, announced that his wife was pregnant. Louise was so distraught that she threatened suicide. When her married boss, Irving, jilted her, she went to his apartment while he was out of town and stole some of his furniture and many of his prized possessions, including a stunning canary diamond ring. Each time she wore that ring, Louise reminded me that one day it would be on my finger. To this day, I hate yellow diamonds.

One of Irving's pieces of furniture, an antique Bombay chest, resided in my childhood home and every house I have occupied since. When I learned the truth of its origin, I sold the chest on Craigslist and gave the money to my mother to make amends for my rotten childhood behavior.

Louise had two Siamese cats named Cee Cee and Coney. Cee Cee was named after Seymour. I was highly allergic, but I wanted to be with Louise so badly that I tolerated the dander and always had an inhaler in hand. Louise would sleep late on Sunday mornings and instruct me not to wake her, even if I was wheezing from the felines. I had to be silent. "Don't sneeze. Don't cough. Don't breathe. Don't speak," she would tell me. I remember that on icy cold mornings I would sit on her balcony overlooking Second Avenue, wrapped in a thin blanket, crying and gasping for air. With tears frozen on my face, I counted the minutes until she would awaken and take me to the children's zoo in Central Park. Like many kids who are mistreated, I ran back to my abuser over and over again. I just wanted to be loved. I remember the time Louise convinced me to steal a heavy gold necklace from my mother's jewelry box. I was eleven.

Me: "Why don't you just ask my mom for the necklace?"

Louise: "You can just take it. She won't know that it is missing. It belongs to me and I want it back. Go get it for me. It's in her bedroom closet in the jewelry box. If you love me you will do it. And don't tell anyone."

I snuck into my mother's closet and found the necklace. I felt sick taking it. I knew it was wrong. I gave it to Louise. I watched my mother search for that chain and charm for years. It was heart-breaking and I felt my head pound with anxiety each time I saw her look, to no avail.

Mom: "Shari, have you seen my necklace? The one with the big gold chai hanging on it? I can't find it."

Me: "No mom. I haven't seen it."

I was now a thief and a liar. Was I a callous criminal or just a miserably needy and misguided kid? Did I crave love so much that I would steal from my own mother?

I never told Mrs. W. about the necklace. How could I? I just prayed for the day I didn't have to go to therapy anymore. As for my mom, I fessed up many years later. And in good mom fashion, she forgave me. I am grateful for her. I am sad for the time we lost as mother and daughter, while I clamored for Louise to love me. I am still haunted by the overnights in Manhattan. To this day, I am afraid of cats. I suppose the worst part of all happened a few years later, when as a teenager I confronted Louise with the things she made me do, the lies I told on her behalf, and the guilt I felt. She was a master gaslighter. "No, no, no, Shari, that never happened. I never said that. You misunderstood me. I love you. You are my favorite," she would say. She succeeded. I thought I was crazy.

But the worst part was the day I finally stood up to her and pushed her out of my life. I was in my late twenties. My paternal grandmother, whom I called Nan, was living with her in Florida, sick with cancer. I wanted to see Nan one last time. I flew down to Fort Lauderdale from New York. My mother picked me up from the airport, and we drove to Cooper City, gifts in hand, to pay our respects to Nan. I got out of the car, walked to the front door, and rang the bell. The door opened a crack.

"What are you doing here?" Louise asked.

"I want to see Nan. Can Mom and I come in please?" I requested.

"No, Nan doesn't want to see you," she said.

From what I knew, based upon my father's reports, Nan was slipping in and out of consciousness.

Why wouldn't she want to see me? She loved me. We had been close my entire life. When she was alert, we spoke on the phone weekly. She was barely able to talk at this point, yet she told Louise that she didn't want to see me? It didn't sound right.

I did everything short of pushing in the door, yet Louise refused to let us past the threshold. Finally, tears in my eyes, Mom and I drove away. I never spoke to Nan again. She died without knowing that I had come to visit.

A week later, my father called to tell me that his mother, my Nan, had passed. Mom and I decided that we should find Jeffrey and let him know. Neither of us had spoken to Jeffrey for a few years since he had abandoned the family. But he should know that his grandmother was gone. Right? When we couldn't locate a phone number for him, we contacted his mother-in-law on a number we found by calling 411.

"Can you please tell Jeffrey that Nan has died. I thought he would want to know," my mother told the lady.

"Oh, thank you," she replied. "But Jeffrey already knows. He was there with her when she passed."

I wasn't privy to the lady's comments, but I watched my mother's face go sheet white, tears welling up in her eyes. She had been searching for Jeffrey, her eldest son, for years, and I remember her crying to Louise on the phone every Sunday about not knowing his whereabouts. It was heartbreaking. Mom dialed the phone and called Louise for the last time.

"You knew where Jeffrey was all along? How could you do that to me? You knew I was trying to find him. You knew how much I hurt. Why would you lie?" Mom pleaded.

"Jeffrey didn't want you to know where he was," Louise said.

"Louise! He's my son. How could you hide him from me?" she cried.

Louise had no answer, but the mystery was solved. She had known where Jeffrey was all along.

Louise was someone who needed to be needed. I had been slowly distancing myself from her since graduating college, when I started to fully comprehend the two decades of her abuse. Sensitive Jeffrey had pulled away from our family years before and was an easy target for her. Louise promised him money, love, security, jewelry, and all of the things she had offered while manipulating me as a kid. Jeffrey fell for it as I once had. Hook, line, and sinker. He had become her new F.A.V.

I grabbed the phone out of my mother's hands.

"Do not EVER call me again Aunt Louise. I hate you. You are a horrible person and a liar. You have hurt Mom, Dad, Jay, and me," I said. "I don't want your jewelry, and I never want to see you again."

The year was 1992. Louise and I never spoke again, but it hasn't stopped hurting. My family lost Jeffrey forever to this evil woman. Louise had power over him the way she had power over me when I was an innocent and trusting child. She was successful in convincing him that we were all damaged. No amount of therapy could heal the relationship with Jeffrey.

Back to my last day at the lake house. Mike told me that he and Bobbi were taking me somewhere special. We would cook and eat on *Spontaneity*, and he would take me somewhere for a big surprise. I faced the back of the boat until we arrived at our destination near the intersection of Mississippi, Alabama, and Tennessee. It was the most beautiful cascade. We were the only ones there. It was our private waterfall!

Bobbi said, "Jump in."

The water was spectacular and the perfect temperature. We donned our water saddles—thick pieces of foam board you mount in the water. We sat and sat and took in the splendor and tranquility of the cove. We drank crafted cocktails, kicked back, and relaxed. I do not think I could have been any happier. I did not want to leave, but as they say, all good things must come to an end.

Bobbi and I drove back to Piperton and ate our last supper together. I cooked linguine with clam sauce. It was magic. Enough garlic to drive the devil away.

On a trip to Italy, I had fallen in love with the linguine and white clam sauce I had ordered at a tiny restaurant located in a small alley. Good thing this chef was also willing to teach me. Most people think they need to use white wine or butter or extra clam juice to make this entree. Not true! Follow this simple recipe, and enjoy this delicious dish!

linguine with white clam sauce

1 box of dry linguine

¼ cup olive oil

head of garlic, minced

¼ cup parsley, minced

2 bags of little neck or top-neck clams (rinsed)

Put olive oil in a heavy stockpot on medium heat. Add minced garlic. Once you smell the garlic, add in the parsley and then the clams. Cover and reduce heat. While the clams are cooking, boil water in a second pot. To the water, add salt and a little olive oil. Cook the linguine in the boiling water according to package instructions. Once the clams are all open, remove from the heat. Pour over strained al dente pasta.

The perfect farewell.

chapter six

go u northwestern!

I kept feeling sad that Jake did not have a proper graduation. Perhaps I could go to Northwestern and take some photos under the arch and surprise him.

"Hello, Michele?"

Michele is my oldest childhood friend. We met as ten-year-old Girl Scouts. We were both put in time-out—it was called detention back then—for talking too much while on a camping trip. Great idea! Take two chatty girls, punish them by putting them on the kitchen floor of Camp Wenasco, and leave them there all night long. Seriously? Did they think we were going to be silent and go to sleep? Did they not remember WHY we were put in time-out?

We became fast friends, laughing, chatting, and telling jokes until dawn. We ultimately fell asleep, clad in our flannel pajamas, and woke up shortly thereafter to a gaggle of gangly orthodonture-sporting, chubby twelve-year-old girls gawking over us. Michele and I were now partners in crime, soul sisters, and forever pals. I must wonder, though, wouldn't the cold, hard kitchen-floor banishment be considered child neglect today? Michele and I still laugh and say, "We could have set the house on fire! What was wrong with them?"

NOTE: According to Michele's mother, Barbara, the appropriate—completely inappropriate—question to screech at someone who behaves like a fool is "WHAT IS WRONG WITH YOU?" Barbara has a unique knack for starting a fight with that one simple query. It stands to reason the target of your rhetorical question will—will not—be, "Well, now that you ask, I have a limp on my left side, adult-onset diabetes, my kids don't speak to me, and I am in debt up to my eyeballs. THAT is what is wrong with me. Thanks for asking!" Terrific way to get a good argument going. Ask people what is wrong with them!

"Michele, can I come visit you in Chicago?" I asked.

"Absolutely!" she said.

I bought a ticket. Off to O'Hare.

Michele's husband Kevin had left for Singapore to start a new job. Michele would join him as soon as she sold the apartment on Gold Coast. This might be the last time we would see each other for a while, and I wanted some quality time. At Michele's apartment I taught her how to braid and bake challah, and introduced her to a recipe I found on Facebook that has become a family favorite. It's called cloud eggs. Who doesn't love a recipe with only two ingredients?

---

cloud eggs

8 eggs

½ cup shredded parmesan cheese

Preheat oven to 450 degrees.

Crack eight eggs, separating the yolks from the whites. Whip the whites with a high-speed mixer until foamy peaks form. Fold in parmesan cheese. Put parchment paper on a large baking sheet. Spoon out the whites to make eight clouds on the baking sheet. Take the back of a tablespoon and make a well in each cloud. You should not see the parchment paper underneath. Put in the oven for about five minutes. Watch carefully. You want the rim of each cloud to be slightly browned.

Remove from the oven. Gently spoon one yolk onto each cloud. Return to the oven for three minutes or until you can see a slight film over the yolks. You do not want the yolks to cook. You are just heating them up. Think of a soft-boiled or poached egg.

You want the yolks runny. Remove from the oven and serve immediately. For extra zest, add truffle salt! You can also add cooked, crumbled dry bacon to the clouds at the same time you fold in the cheese. Enjoy!

After a few days of staring at the walls of Michele's brownstone, we decided to use one of the certificates I had purchased at a trade show to stay at London House Hotel on the Chicago River. I LOVE the Chicago River, especially when they dye it neon green for St. Patrick's Day. I had had the pleasure of experiencing this phenomenon a year before when my friends Clint and Adam got married. I love gay weddings.

"Shari, I can't go to the hotel with you. I lost my wallet! I can't find it anywhere. I know it slipped out of my bag,'" Michele said.

I was 100 percent positive that her wallet was at home. Michele only THINKS she loses things, but she never actually does. When I am with her, we spend a lot of time playing hide-and-seek with her glasses, wallet, water bottle, keys, pens, and credit cards. I knew that if I didn't overreact and just kept quiet for about thirty minutes, Michele would find her wallet, and we would be on our way to the hotel. Winner chicken dinner!

We took an Uber to London House. It was the first time I had been inside a hotel since December. Everything was spotless. There was a seal of cleanliness sticker on the door to our room. We entered with caution. It was dark. The drapes were closed. Zip! I retracted the curtains. The sun streamed in. I saw the Chicago River below. It was deep blue and glistening. I looked across the street.

HOLY SHIT! This could not be for real. A dead-on view of a HUGE golden Trump sign emblazoned on the front of the Donald's hotel. There had been a mistake. I picked up the phone.

"Hello? This is Shari Wallack. I am having an issue in my room, and I need to move."

"What is the issue?" asked the lady on the other end of the phone.

"I cannot look at the Trump sign across the street. Can't I escape politics at this hotel? I don't want to see the name of any presidential candidate when I open the curtains," I exclaimed.

"Well, Ms. Wallack," she said, "all of our view rooms have the same view. I can move you a few flights down, and you can look up at him. Or I can move you a few flights up, and you can look down on him. Which would you prefer?"

I didn't want to look up or down at anyone. I just wanted to enjoy the spectacular and expansive view of Chicago. I might as well just stay put, facing it head-on. It was only for two days, and I would go out for long walks.

Michele and I spent a week together. She and my Aunt Helen had been my inspiration for learning mah-jongg last year, so we played it at least an hour a day. Crack! Bam! Dot! You know the drill if you play the game. It had helped me with my anxiety when I was home, so why not try it on the road? It is hard to be anxious when you are attempting to read the card, pong and kung yourself silly, while avoiding a discard of the wrong dragon ruining your hand. I don't play nearly as well as Rachel in *Crazy Rich Asians*, so if I threw the opponent's winning tile, I would never know!

I decided while in Chicago to make a bucket list. I had traveled the world, put two kids through college, started a company, won awards, and finally bought my dream apartment in New York City. What was left? Let's see. Oh, I know! I want to write a book once I figure out the topic. Oprah's Book Club! I dream of being a guest on the *Today Show* or *CBS Sunday Morning*, but for what fabulous achievement? It's not as if I am going to win the Nobel Prize anytime soon. Oh! I've got it! I want to teach a class at an accredited university. That's it! Teach a class! But where?

I had recently seen that Florida State University opened the new Jim Moran School of Entrepreneurship. That was perfect. I sent an email to their administration. The following day I got a reply from Shelly Griffin, one of the faculty.

"Yes! We would love to have you teach a Zoom session on branding, marketing, and selling," she said. "You can teach the 9:05 a.m. and the 1:25 p.m. sessions."

I picked September 16. I had no idea where I would be on that date, but I like to check boxes and get things over with. Otherwise, there is a chance I will chicken out. I did not want to chicken out! I just needed to figure out what to say on September 16. I had never taught a class before. That would be my little secret.

Michele agreed to drive with me to Evanston so that I could take some photos under the Northwestern Arch on Deering Lawn, and in front of Andy's, the iconic campus custard shop. Andy's was so famous that Rachel had written her college entrance essay about it. They make concretes, which are akin to the Dairy Queen Blizzard, but way better.

I had sent an email a few weeks earlier to Morton "Morty" Shapiro, the university president. I had an opportunity to meet him electronically during both kids' tenure at the school. When you pay upwards of $75k a year per kid, Morty will reply to your messages. I met him outside Deering Library that day after he filmed some wear-your-mask public service announcements.

"Hi, Morty!" I shouted across Deering Lawn.

"Hi, Shari," he replied with a smile. "Let's go take some photos under the arch."

GREAT. We walked over to the arch. I inquired, "How are things going for you during COVID? It must be difficult for you."

He replied, "Not as difficult as it is for the parents of the incoming freshmen."

I was saying a little gratitude prayer that both of my kids had graduated before COVID. We walked over to the arch and took a few photos with the colorful signs I had made.

Would Morty be willing to record a short video to personally congratulate Jake on his graduation?

He certainly was! There is a good chance I have the only video of its kind.

A personalized message from Morty:

"Hey, Jake! This is Morty Shapiro underneath this mask, hat, and sunglasses. I just want to tell you that I am proud of you. Congratulations. I know you are going to make the world a better place. Go Cats!"

I was elated. I had a video with Morty. I had photos of all over the campus. Jake's last apartment building. Jake's favorite bubble tea stop. The barbershop. Far too many Asian and Indian restaurants. His favorite hangouts. Last stop? Andy's! I wanted a photo and a concrete! My mouth was watering.

Michele and I arrived, and there it was. The sign. My heart hurt. "Due to COVID, we had to make the difficult decision to permanently close Andy's. Thank you for your support for the past twelve years." NO!!!! Andy's? COVID closed Andy's? I was devastated when I found out they had closed the Tenement Museum in New York City and my favorite sushi restaurant in Fort

Lauderdale. But Andy's? This was going to be my last concrete for a long time, and I was not going to get it. Ever. RIP Andy, whoever you are.

As I was packing to leave Chicago, Michele handed me a tiny bag with a gift inside. It was a miniature red dragon mah-jongg tile with a tiny red bell. She had bought several when she was in Asia. I immediately attached it to my Scenic backpack. This was my new lucky charm. Bam!

who can turn the world on with a smile?

Minneapolis! The land of wild rice, ten thousand lakes, the Mall of America, and Mary!

When I was a young girl of eight, I would sit in front of the television, Saturday nights, 8:00 p.m., CBS, for half an hour of Mary Tyler Moore and the rest of the cast. I loved everything about the show. I disappeared into it. I had had a manipulative and mentally abusive childhood at the hands of my paternal aunt and grandmother. Mary made me forget my troubles for thirty minutes once a week. She was better than any therapist! Now, in 2020, I had to see the Mary house from the show's prologue, and I needed to visit the Mary statue. So many memories flooded back. At the statue at 700 Nicolette Mall, I linked arms with Mary and sang the theme song for everyone in the street.

Mary could turn the world on with her smile. She could make something out of a nothing day. If love was truly all around, I was going to find it, give it, and find purpose in it. The lyrics to that 70s sitcom song had more meaning for me. Smile. Spread joy. Make the most of each day. Give freely. Expect nothing in return. Don't waste a minute. Live! Take on this town and each one that follows.

Shari, you are not just going to make it. You are going to soar. Thank you, Mary!

I spent the first few days of my Minnesota escape with my friend Doreen, who lives in an adorable suburb of Minneapolis. We rented e-bikes, went for walks, entertained her Chihuahua, Mr. Black—well, he was a black male dog. It just fit. He came with the name.

We went to visit the George Floyd memorial. Along the way, we saw many burned-out buildings, smashed and boarded-up windows, closed businesses, and empty streets. I had seen financial ruin in New York and Chicago, but this was the scene of the crime, the beginning of a movement, the very spot where Gianna Floyd lost her dad. Outside the convenience store where Floyd apparently tried to pass a counterfeit $20.

The spot where Officer Chauvin kneeled on Floyd's neck for eight minutes and forty-six seconds.

The place where Floyd uttered the haunting words, "I can't breathe!" The memorial reminded me of the one erected in Parkland, Florida, following the Valentine's Day massacre of 2018. As in Parkland, Florida, there were notes, cards, flowers, artwork, and multimedia displays. A chalk drawing of an angel replaced Floyd's dead body on the asphalt outside the store. A young Black girl was singing "This Girl is on Fire" on an endless loop at the top of her lungs. Free COVID tests were being administered. My friends and I took one. Pamphlets and water bottles were distributed. Visitors were silent.

As far as the eye could see, painted on the ground, were the names of Black lives lost to police violence. Dozens of names. It was daunting. It was not just a memorial to George Floyd but a tribute to Breonna Taylor, Trayvon Martin, Ahmaud Arbery, Michael Brown, Tamir Rice, and the many others senselessly killed. Change has got to happen. Enough is enough.

With tears in our eyes and heavy hearts, we left the memorial. On our car ride back to Doreen's house, we sat in silence.

When we got home, Doreen asked me to teach her to make challah bread. She had seen me do it on Facebook, and it now was her turn. Her brand-new oven was not working. We prepared the dough but had to walk it across the street to her neighbor's house. George and Mark are a disabled gay couple who spend all day, every day, smoking pot and eating pot brownies. Their house looked as if it was being prepared for an estate sale. There were knickknacks everywhere. Every inch of wall space and cabinet space was overrun with collected artwork, including a wall draped in bright blue felt and adorned with antique rhinestone brooches. Yes! Brooches. It was like a drag queen fantasy!

We placed the challah into their oven. How much more bread could I consume? I had already put on ten pounds, munching on challah in the last several cities. While we waited for the bread to bake, Doreen showed me around the gardens. Plants everywhere! A koi pond. Vegetables wildly growing and left unpicked. While outside, I could smell the marijuana that was burning inside the house. Wait! Maybe I could smell it IN the garden? Oh my goodness!

The tallest cannabis plants I had ever seen. The scent was pervasive and fresh! George came out and explained how he harvested marijuana and the process involved in baking it into edibles. I was thinking, I just need to sit in the garden and I will get high, but maybe an edible would be fun.

"Got a brownie for me?" I asked George.

"Sure, here you go," he replied without hesitation.

I wanted to pop it in my mouth, but Doreen stopped me. "You cannot eat this until you go to bed. Trust me, this is serious stuff," she warned.

Okay, I would wait 'til bedtime.

We decided to watch a movie after dinner. *The Bird Cage* was a favorite of ours, so we turned it on. Doreen handed me half a brownie.

"Is half enough?" I questioned.

"You probably only need a quarter," she replied.

Okay, we each had a half. Having never eaten one before, I had no idea how long it would take to work.

After thirty minutes, I turned to Doreen and said, "This is not working! I didn't eat enough."

"Wait a little while longer!" she exclaimed.

We kept watching the movie, and the funny scenes got funnier. We were belly laughing. Mr. Black had a noxious gas attack. We laughed even harder. Even the most innocuous lines seemed hilarious. I was high as a kite, as if I were back in high school when I had smoked pot at the cast parties of the various plays and musicals I performed in. I felt the room begin to spin. I could not get up. I was out of control.

I do not remember how I got up the steep staircase and into bed that night. Once tucked in, I did not move. The room continued to spin. I could not focus. I was afraid to fall on the way to the bathroom, so I held it in all night.

Monday morning, Doreen dropped me off at the home of a former client and lifelong friend, Judy. I have known her, her husband Jeff, and their boys Drew and Neil for more than twenty years. As empty nesters, Judy and Jeff were happy to have some company. While Judy worked, I tooled around in the kitchen.

My challah was a hit. Judy joked that Jeff considered an entire challah as a dinner roll! I never saw anyone eat so much bread in one sitting. I was happy he enjoyed it.

The highlight of my visit with them was a trip to Minnesota's Largest Candy Store. No, that is not the description. That is the name of the place! Minnesota's Largest Candy Store. And it did not disappoint. They did not have just an enormous selection of candy. They had every candy I had ever eaten. Ever! Candy buttons on steroids, candy necklaces, Valentine heart candies, licorice tacos, Disney-themed Pez dispensers with every flavor pellet, jellybeans, gummies, cookies, chocolate! It was grounds for a diabetic coma! They also had strange soda and beer flavors; most I had never seen before. My head was spinning. I was gaining weight with every inhale.

And they did not have just American items. There were rows of Asian cookies and candy, French, Swiss, and German chocolate, and an entire aisle of bread mixes, salad dressings, and other specialty items. I quickly purchased over $100 worth of kiddie treats to send to my North Carolina cousins while I gobbled up some Japanese sugar wafers. Yum!

How could candy be enough? How about ice cream? Sure! We went to a specialty house-made gelato place, and I ate black licorice custard. Yeah. It was as weird as it sounds. It was black, sweet, and tasted like Sambuca, minus the coffee bean and the fire, which I had enjoyed on my trips to Italy. I could eat only half and tossed the rest. Enough sugar for one night. Tomorrow was another day. I think next time I will stick to mocha chip!

After a few days of Jeff's freezing me out of the house—he liked to keep the place at sixty-five—I was collected by Dan, also a former client who had become a close friend and confidante. Let me explain Dan. Squirrel. Got it? Full-on ADD but kind, caring, funny, and adventurous. Dan and his wife Silva are up for everything and anything. First stop? The supermarket, of course. I was set to cook for them for an entire week. We planned menus for both their house in Roseville and the townhouse in Tofte up on Lake Superior.

We rode e-bikes, sat on the patio around the gas firepit, and gazed at the stars while listening to James Taylor, Carole King, and Kenny Loggins. My kind of people! We made challah that first night, and I taught them the Jewish prayer. They loved it.

Dan showed me some of the projects he had been working on since retirement. He can make work benches, flower boxes, coasters, and nature chains, my favorite. Nature chains are like mobiles, constructed out of copper wire, wood, rocks, colored gemstones, and sea glass. I wanted to ask him for one but was afraid he would say no.

Dan is a social media addict. I can absolutely relate. He loves to read and comment on posts, pass along his political views, and share photos of Shakira—his dream girl. The most special thing Dan posts is on Sunday morning. Each Sunday, he shares a photo of a coffee mug. He has dozens of them. It's a different one each week. Some are from his travels; some have funny sayings, and some are just pretty or unique. Having coffee on a Sunday is especially enjoyable if Dan joins you.

On Sunday, August 30, we set out for Tofte, a four-hour drive from Roseville. I felt like a kid, an only child, on vacation with her parents. They bickered, and I sat in the back seat, hoping that this mommy and daddy were not getting a divorce! We stopped at a seafood market to purchase smoked fish, which is a big deal in Minnesota. While there, I noticed the bags of wild rice. I had never had Minnesota wild rice, which I found out later is not rice at all. It is a grain. It grows in the lake on reeds and is harvested by beating the reeds on the ground, at which point the grains fall off. The best wild rice is not the kind that is pitch black. It is brownish and somewhat spotted. It is delicious!

Easy to make: one cup of rice to three cups of broth or water. Add a teaspoon of butter or olive oil. Cook in a covered casserole dish at 375 degrees for about an hour, or until all the liquid is absorbed. Serve with everything.

"How do you feel about fishing?" Dan asked me.

"I love to fish. I am enthralled by fishing," I said.

Actually, there is only one person in my life who is truly enthralled by fishing. My dad. He used to wake me up at 5:00 a.m. on Sunday mornings to go fishing with him on party boats all over Long Island. Port Jefferson, Montauk, Freeport. Anywhere and everywhere. I hated waking up early, making tuna fish sandwiches, driving an hour or more to get to the pier, baiting the hook, pretending to enjoy it, and vomiting from seasickness in the toilet of the tiny head in the belly of the boat. But I wanted to hang out with my father, and this is what he liked to do when he wasn't working or watching football, basketball, ice hockey, and baseball in our living room or at the stadium. If I had to make a choice, fishing was the lesser of two evils.

Sports were agony. So, I sucked it up and went fishing with Dad frequently throughout my childhood. As much as I disliked fishing, I turned out to be quite proficient. I'll admit that eventually I even learned to tolerate it.

"Enthralled by fishing" is actually a quote from a different family story. My maternal grandmother, Esther Strassner, passed at eighty-six from pancreatitis. She got sick after eating a hot dog at Jake's sixth birthday party in our backyard. She was rushed to the hospital by ambulance and died before she knew what had hit her. When the rent-a-rabbi from the funeral home called us in to discuss her life and get material for the service to take place the following day, Aunt Helen mentioned that Grammy Esther would go fishing with Poppa Joe on their boat in Shinnecock. My mom, uncle, and I chimed in that she also liked to do crossword puzzles, wrap gifts for the Hadassah Valentine's Day parties at her condo in Hallandale, cut her own curly hair, and play chopsticks on the piano.

The funeral began. The benches were filled with walker-dependent octogenarians donning polyester. It was solemn and quiet. I imagined the attendees wondering when their time would be up. Not five minutes into the service, after the perfunctory "Friends, we are gathered here to celebrate the life of Esther Strassner," the hired clergy uttered these words: "Esther liked to fish with her husband Joe. She loved fishing. In fact, Esther was enthralled by fishing." My entire family burst out in laughter.

Enthralled? Did he just say that? She tolerated it at best. She probably didn't like it at all. She did it to spend time with my grandfather the same way I did it to spend time with my dad. I didn't realize how much we had in common.

As a joke and a way to help us get over our grief, Aunt Helen found, copied, framed, and gifted everyone in our immediate family with the one existing photo of Grammy Esther sitting on the boat, fishing pole in hand, actually enjoying a day on the Long Island Sound.

Back to Tofte. I wanted to spend time with Dan, and he wanted to fish. Sound familiar? I was going to suck it up as I had done when I was a kid. Maybe fresh-water fishing on a private boat would be my thing?

"Fishing? When can we go?" I asked with trepidation.

Dan chartered a boat and captain, and off we went. It was cold, and the lake was extremely choppy.

Isn't it only choppy on the ocean? Clearly, I wasn't a lake expert.

Good thing I hadn't eaten, or it would have been like that scene in *Stand by Me* when Fat Ass drinks a bottle of castor oil and swallows a raw egg before the pie-eating contest. Not a good moment for Fat Ass!

This was hardly fishing. The captain released the lines of eight fishing rods, put them in holsters, and then told us when to reel in the fish. I did get to reel in a few, including a king salmon. Yes! A king salmon in Lake Superior. How awesome. King salmon was the exception to the "I don't like salmon" rule. The rest of our bounty was a handful of lake trout which were super fun to catch. We snagged five in total. The captain filleted them on the dock, and we put them in the freezer, except for the salmon, which I insisted we eat that night. I have never eaten fresher fish. It was delicious, with Minnesota wild rice of course!

My time in Minnesota had come to an end. I was sad to leave, but eager to face my next adventure. I was feeling better and more alive. My anxiety and depression were tapering off, but I was at odds with my parents and was not quite sure where I stood with my children. I was keeping my distance for fear of saying something that would completely ruin any of those relationships. I just did not want to be controlled or told what to do. Spending time with friends and avoiding difficult conversations had been a good and healthy escape.

I was posting my adventures on social media for anyone who wanted to see what I was doing. My technologically inept father, and those who weren't Facebook fans would have to wait for a personal recounting of my journey. I had shared my frustrations with a trusted relative, whom I also consider a close friend. I told her that I was happy with the distance, both physically and emotionally.

I received this email:

Shari,

If you do not want to get upset—Don't Read This!!!

The easiest way to get my attention.

You are not going to like what I am about to say!!!! Sorry!!!!

I may not like it, but I am going to see what she has to say.

No one wants to be judged, disrespected, or reprimanded. It appears your kids are unhappy with YOU, and you are unhappy with them. You are unhappy with your parents. Should everyone "pull a Jeffrey" to be happy?

She just had to throw in Jeffrey. That was low. My overly-sensitive, middle-child-syndrome brother went to school to become a psychologist, analyzed our entire family, and disappeared with his wife and two daughters decades ago. He never tried to work it out. He abandoned everyone. I was just taking a mental health break!

Running away is a temporary fix, and at some point, you have two choices: Eliminate everyone who causes stress in your life, or suck it up because people don't change and they don't appreciate your critical analysis of them. They do not have to be who YOU want them to be.

I wonder. YOU have a difficult relationship with your family, but a marvelous relationship with outsiders. Spend the rest of your life cooking and baking for strangers? Really, Shari? Get real! I guess you can run away forever, keep putting your pictures on Facebook for love and validation, or go home and try to find some way to cope. No one wants to talk to you? So, are they making you more miserable, or are you making them more miserable?

This is a horrible situation, and it appears you must stop filling your time and escaping into things that will not matter and get back to the things that will.

You may be traveling, but you are really lost. I am sorry to get you upset, and I know you are looking for love and support.

It hurts me to send this. Still love you!

Initially, I was shocked at what she had to say. I knew she loved me, and it must have been hard to send that message.

Was she right? Was I running? Was I the problem? Should I go home and fix everything?

Wait! This was the best I had felt in years. I was not crying. I was thriving. I was not being controlled or controlling anyone else. I was seeing this spectacular country on my own terms. I was taking "me" time. I had faced my fears of traveling alone. I faced my anxiety of driving by myself for more than an hour or two. This journey was EXACTLY what I needed.

After a few minutes, I responded:

Lost? Far from it. I chose to surround myself with people who are kind and not judgmental, disrespectful, unappreciative, rude, or hurtful.

My parents have narcissistic tendencies and a lack of respect for my wishes or feelings. My children are off on their own journeys, and I am doing my best to help them to grow and find their way. I have done all I can for them.

There are people in the world who are kind, and I want to be around them. I escaped Florida to clear my head and remove some of the pressure I was feeling. Perhaps you cannot relate.

I did not get much help growing up. I had to figure it out . . . all while being manipulated and hurt, lied to, deceived, and somewhat neglected. I cannot speak to either of my parents right now about that because it will frustrate me further.

Did you feel better sending that message and comparing me to Jeffrey? I hardly think there is a comparison there. For now, I will be on the road, "getting real."

Then I received this reply:

I hear you. I thought you wanted my input. I have to say what I think, even if it is not what you want to hear or believe. I am sorry you didn't like what you read, but that's my opinion, and we can agree to disagree. None of us can fix the past or change people around us. Of course, we are all free to leave. If you choose to seek out and be happy with only those who make you happy, that's your choice. If you do that, I think you also choose the consequences, whatever they will be.

The past catches up to all of us, even you. You have problems with your kids, just like your parents had problems with their kids. Your kids wish you had treated them differently, and you wish they treated you differently. It's a mess!

Maybe you think there is no comparison to Jeffrey, but he couldn't take it and left to clear his head too. He was happier with those outside of the family, as you are, and it seems your kids are too. I wish you safety and peace as you pursue happiness. I still believe there is no place like home. Life is full of good and bad. Nothing is solved by running away.

A few hours passed, and I decided it would be best to pick up the phone. I was not angry. I was grateful for the opportunity to explain this journey to her. I imagine that to the outside, it looked like a senseless escape from home. For me, it was more of a reset. It was a chance to take a break, but also to give others a break from me. I was certain. I was not going to stop anytime soon.

oh boise!

*I*f you are familiar with the Mormon religion, you know that their growth comes from producing large families in addition to their work as missionaries. The latter involves sending young members of the church (Church of Jesus Christ of Latter-day Saints) away from their hometowns to educate fledgling outsiders about the benefits of their religion. Those who are looking for meaning, purpose, and a sense of belonging are perfect prospects.

When Mormon missionaries rang my doorbell in the past, I invited them in, served them matzo ball soup, and told them that they, too, could be "chosen" if they agreed to convert to Judaism. Wouldn't that make Heavenly Father happy? I have not had much success. Jews are not the best recruiters. Truth is, if you are not one of us, you must go through quite a process to join. You find us; we do not find you.

Ten years ago, while attending the Direct Selling Association annual conference, I had been introduced to Orville and Heidi Thompson, the founders of a quickly growing, direct-selling company called Scentsy. They manufacture warmers that work with the heat of light bulbs to melt wax cubes. This process produces dozens of glorious scents that waft throughout your home and office. The multilevel marketing concept consists of people selling to people—and now via the internet—and recruiting other people to market the goods. Those at the top are paid on the products they sell, as well as those that their downline—sales organization—sells. Leaders at the top of the chain are exceptionally well-compensated and win fabulous incentive travel trips, which is what Buy the Sea organizes and manages.

Back to Scentsy. The Thompsons were hundreds of thousands of dollars in debt following the events of September 11, 2001. They had owned a company where the business model was to sell products at state fairs and other expos. At that time, hundreds of thousands of dollars' worth of items were on order that could not be canceled. The same volume of product was in hand and could not be sold because customers weren't traveling to their booths. No one was buying.

Orville and Heidi had landed in a rough spot. As is typical for members of the church, they had five young children. The Thompsons needed a quick fix and some instant cash.

In 2004, while manning their own sales booth selling various products, Orville Thompson met a pair of ladies selling chunks of candle wax melted in electric warmers under the brand name Scentsy. Heidi and Orville needed a new venture, and the ladies needed someone to grow their idea. The Thompsons purchased Scentsy from these women and built what is now one of the most successful direct-selling companies on record. In 2020, the pandemic forced millions of people to work from home. Other than my Aunt Helen, who is allergic to fragrances, who doesn't want their home to smell nice? Quarantine brought Scentsy and the Thompsons even greater success!

Back to the story. Even though I had gotten to know Heidi and Orville throughout the years, I had not been successful in convincing them to work with Buy the Sea. Enter Eldon Gale. Eldon was living in Columbus, working for Nationwide Insurance. Although he loved the job as director of events, the company wasn't the best fit for him. He was a member of the church and therefore not a social after-hours drinker. He was open to a change, and one that would bring him closer to his family in eastern Washington state. He deserved a community that would embrace him, his wife Tricia, and their four children, Maxwell, Jackson, Claire, and Annie.

While in the insurance industry, Eldon had successfully worked with our team at Buy the Sea. If he were to leave Nationwide, we hoped that he would take us with him to the next company.

In June of 2014, Caryn and I were walking down the halls of the annual DSA show and spotted Orville, Heidi, and Orville's brother Chuck. We exchanged pleasantries. Heidi mentioned that they were looking for a new director of incentive travel. BINGO!

"You have got to hire Eldon Gale!" I said.

Chuck looked at Orville. "Gale?" he asked. "Where is he from?"

"Eastern Washington state," I replied.

The Thompsons were also from Washington. Chuck and Orville proceeded to play a game that I call Jewish geography, the Mormon edition.

"Don't we know the Gales?" Chuck asked.

Mormon families are WAY bigger than their Jewish counterparts, so if they played the game long enough, surely the Thompsons either knew the Gales or were related to them. I was just praying they would hire a Gale. And a few months later, they did!

Eldon had been asking me to come to Boise every year thereafter. With my extensive travel and kid responsibilities, I'd never found the time to visit. But now I needed my next destination. I was not ready to go back to Plantation.

"Hello, Eldon? How do you feel about a visit? I want to come to Boise!" I stated.

"Sure! When are you coming?" he asked.

"Well, how do you feel about attending a virtual bar mitzvah with me?" I replied.

"Wow! I would love to. Can Trish and the kids participate?" he asked.

"Of course! I will come to you on September 4, and we will watch my cousin Joey's bar mitzvah in your living room on the fifth!" I told him.

Eldon and Tricia picked me up at the airport.

"Do you have bread flour? Got eggs, vegetable oil, sugar, yeast, and salt?" I asked at 9:00 p.m.

"Well, we have everything except the bread flour, but our neighbor Bonnie will lend us some," Tricia said.

"Great, we will need to get it by 7:30 a.m. so that I can get a challah in the oven in time for the bar mitzvah," I explained. "Oh, and I have a toothache. I might need a root canal," I told them.

"No problem," Tricia replied. "One of our friends is a dentist, well, a pediatric dentist, and he will open up his office for you and take X-rays."

Wow, she called the dentist friend at 10:00 p.m., and he responded. He could see me the next day, Saturday, when their office would be closed. Unheard of where I live.

"Actually," Tricia said, "he will see you now."

"Now? As in at ten on a Friday night? Now?" I asked.

"We do that around here. Everyone helps everyone else," she explained.

So off we drove, down the road to Blair Pediatric Dentistry. Marne—pronounced Mar-nay—and her husband Randy, the dentist, opened the office, sat me in the chair, and took multiple X-rays of my upper right side. We examined the films together. No root damage. Thank goodness! Maybe I was having phantom pain from my corn-nut chomping episode with Michele in Chicago. One evening, after I had taken an Ambien, Michele found me leaning over the kitchen counter, munching extraordinarily hard corn nuts by the handful. When she told me about it the next morning, I had absolutely no recollection.

Note to self: when taking Ambien, go immediately to bed. Do not pass GO. Do not collect $200.

Before leaving the dentist's office, I asked, "What do I owe you?"

"Nothing," Randy said.

Nothing? If I tried this stunt at home and called a dentist on a Friday night, a few things would have happened. First, I would not have gotten a reply. Second, if they agreed to open the office on Saturday, which would have been unlikely, I would have been charged for the X-rays AND a surcharge for an after-hours visit. These Boise people were super nice. Could I just leave, or would they ask me to join the church?

When we returned to the Gales' home, I was escorted upstairs to Claire's room. There, I would spend the next nine nights. Claire loves pineapples. She is eleven. Pineapples? If I were going to list my favorite décor themes, I promise you that pineapple would be low on the list. If I had to list my favorite fruits in descending order, pineapple would be near the bottom, next to apricot. I hate apricots. It's the only fruit you should not serve me if I come to your house.

I went to bed with visions of pineapples dancing in my head, just like "'Twas the Night Before Christmas," with pineapples replacing the sugar plums.

On Saturday, September 5, I woke up, took a shower, and put on the only outfit I had that was fitting for a bar mitzvah, a cute white dress with black and pink flowers that I had picked up in downtown Minneapolis a few weeks earlier. I had exploded out of most of the clothes I had packed for this trip. Challah = belly fat. This dress accommodated my newly enhanced girth, and it was dressier than stretch pants, the only other thing I could fit into.

The Gales gathered with me around the television. The Mormons were embracing the Jews and enjoying the service. If you have been to a bar mitzvah, and you are not a relative or close family friend, it is not generally enjoyable. The bar mitzvah boy—or bat mitzvah girl—is either very prepared, making it tolerable, or completely ill-prepared, making it an extraordinarily long and painful experience. Thank goodness Joey was wonderful and well-rehearsed. I was so proud of him.

It was great to see my cousins and aunt and uncle on the screen. There were only nine people in attendance at the synagogue in Toledo, Ohio—you know, of Jamie Farr fame. Klinger from *MASH*? One of the main attractions in Toledo is a place called Tony Packo's, where you eat Hungarian hot dogs with chili. I wonder if that place survived COVID.

While Joey said the prayer over the challah, the Gale family and I did the same.

Baruch atah Adonai, Eloheinu melech ha'olam. Hamotzi lechem min ha'aretz. Amen.

Blessed are You, Adonai, our G-d, Sovereign of all, who brings forth bread from the earth. Amen.

The Gales loved the challah, and together we inhaled the entire bread quickly. Off to the grocery store to buy more bread flour.

"Could we add things into the challah?" Eldon asked.

Of course, we could! In addition to the bread flour, I bought sun-dried tomatoes, pine nuts, herbes de Provence, coconut, chocolate chips, Oreo cookie crumbles, food coloring, slivered almonds, and parmesan cheese. We were going to have some fun!

In addition to returning flour to Bonnie, we were going to bring her some bread. And we would do the same to thank Dr. Randy and Marne for helping me the night before.

The Gale challah shop was in business.

First up? Sun-dried tomato, pine nut, herb, parmesan. Second? Almond Joy! I could not call it coconut, almond, chocolate chip, graham cracker, Oreo cookie bread. Too complicated. What if we dyed it blue, pink, and purple! Unicorn had to be in the name. Okay, Almond Joy Unicorn bread!

Once they were baked and cooled, Tricia and I delivered some to Marne and then Bonnie. Marne posted the following message on Facebook:

When your friend has a Jewish friend visiting and needs you to give her a tooth X-ray, always say YES! This homemade challah bread is to d(y)e for!

I was SO happy. My heart and my head were healing. The next day, I did a FaceTime class to show Marne and some of the other neighbors how to make this delicious bread on their own. Later that afternoon, Marne posted the following with a photo of her daughter: "Our first try. Thanks, Shari Wallack, for the virtual lesson."

Others saw it and wanted to know how to make it. Was there not a single Jew in Boise?

Eldon said, "I bet we are the only ones in Idaho making challah bread!"

I thought, perhaps we are not the only ones making challah bread, but we are certainly the only ones making Almond Joy Unicorn bread!

Later that day, Tricia's friend Carmen came by to deliver dinner for the kids because Eldon, Tricia, and I had been invited to have dinner with Orville and Heidi at a new restaurant called Crave. In walked Carmen with a Crock-Pot full of chicken chili and tortilla chips.

"Does this happen on a regular basis?" I asked Tricia.

"Sort of. When a family needs a meal, another family knows, and they just provide it," she explained.

Really? In my neighborhood we do not even know each other, and we certainly do not know if someone needs a meal. And even if we did, we don't bring them one. It just does not work like that in Plantation, Florida. It did not work like that where I grew up in New Hyde Park, New York, either. People kept to themselves. Closed doors. Secrets. This was quite a pleasant surprise. I found out that Carmen is a massage therapist and works out of her house down the block.

A massage! I could use one of those. I booked one for the next day for ninety minutes. She charged me $90 and was exceptionally talented! I asked if I could come back again a few days later. During that massage I said, "Please keep going until you get every knot out of me." The session lasted two and a half hours. I was lucky to get a third one in before leaving Boise. I wish Carmen could travel around with me! She is also the friend who lent the Gales a Keurig for my stay. Otherwise, I would have had to trek to Starbuck each morning for a caffeine hit! I find it a little strange that Mormons can drink as much Coke and Dr. Pepper as they want, full of caffeine, but coffee and tea are off the table. Some things I just embrace and accept.

We met Orville and Heidi at 7:15 p.m. at Crave. A little backstory. Scentsy had booked a Bermuda cruise for twenty-two hundred incentive winners and their guests to sail on the Royal Caribbean Adventure of the Seas in June 2020. When COVID hit, there was doubt that the cruise would take place. March turned into April, then May. If Scentsy just waited it out, they would get a full refund of their purchase price. June arrived, and the sailing was canceled. The client was given two options: get the money back or take a 125 percent future cruise credit to be used in 2022. Sadly, Eldon was advised by the executive team to take a refund.

At this time, we were losing programs daily. This was a multimillion-dollar deal. We did not want to give up. Royal Caribbean did not want us to give up either. What if we could offer Scentsy a seven-night Alaska cruise in July 2022 at the same price as the Bermuda cruise that had just been canceled? With incredible rates and that extra 25 percent value—we were able to do it! We asked our rep, Frank Robleto, to pull something together. Scentsy could operate the Alaska program in peak season 2022, for LESS than their 2020 Bermuda program. They would even have credit left over to take additional guests to Alaska or run a second cruise to a different destination. BINGO!

But we still could not convince Scentsy to take the deal. Were they afraid to lose their investment? After all, Royal Caribbean ships were not sailing, and there was no real return to service date. What if we had RCCL put the money into an Escrow account? We presented that idea, and still, no deal. Finally, we put the refund wheels in motion. I felt like a failure. At least we still had a good relationship with Eldon, the Thompsons, and the Scentsy team. When things returned to normal, there would be more opportunities.

Dinner at Crave was fantastic. It was so good to see Orville and Heidi. We spent a few hours talking about their kids, the two upcoming family weddings, and their first grandbaby on the way. Exciting!

Not intending to make a sales pitch, I interjected some of the deals I was making and how the cruise lines were offering never-to-be-seen-again pricing. With that, Orville turned to Eldon and asked, "So where are we with our incentives?"

Eldon said, "Well, we requested a refund for the Bermuda cruise. RCCL did offer some great rates for Alaska, but you declined."

"How good of a deal was it?" asked Orville.

I am a salesperson. I know when someone's interest has been piqued. Orville was interested.

"Eldon has the proposal," I said. "Would you like to see it?" Before he could answer, I pulled out two Ziploc baggies of freshly made challah bread. "Do you like bread?" I asked.

"Sure!" exclaimed Heidi. "What kind of bread?"

I shared, "I have Almond Joy Unicorn and sun-dried tomato, herbes de Provence, pine nut, parmesan. It doesn't have a name yet. Want some?" Their eyes grew bigger. "Can I teach you the Jewish prayer over the bread?" I asked.

"Sure!" they said in unison.

Baruch atah Adonai, Eloheinu melech ha'olam. Hamotzi lechem min ha'aretz. Amen.

Blessed are You, Adonai, our G-d, Sovereign of all, who brings forth bread from the earth. Amen.

"Try some," I said. "Start with the savory and move on to the sweet."

Orville and Heidi were in challah heaven. "You MADE this?" they asked.

"Yes!" I said. "I can teach you! Would you like that?"

"Absolutely!" Heidi exclaimed. "What are you doing tomorrow night?"

"Nothing," I replied.

"Come on over!" Heidi said.

"Would you like me to teach a Jewish cooking class?" I asked.

"We would love that. I like falafel with those special pickles and hummus!" Orville added. "Come to our place at 6:00 p.m., and we will cook together. Sarah loves truffles! Can you make a bread with truffles?" Orville requested.

"You bet I can!" I stated. Hmm, truffle bread? I had absolutely no idea if I could make truffle bread, but I was sure going to try!

The following day I went shopping. I bought everything we needed to make multiple loaves of bread with all kinds of ingredients. I bought enough items to fill a dozen grocery-store bags: a chicken, chicken broth, vegetables, pita, hummus, falafel, ricotta cheese, eggs, truffle oil, parmesan, sour cream, berries, and matzo meal. I arrived at the Thompsons' house at 6:00 p.m. sharp! I felt like the housekeeper, pulling up in Tricia's Honda Odyssey, unloading the family groceries in front of their lovely house with its most magnificent landscaping.

Orville, Heidi, and a few family members were waiting. It was to be my first in-person cooking class, but they did not have to know that!

THE MENU

falafel in pita with lettuce, tomato, israeli pickles, and hummus

chicken soup with melt-in-your-mouth matzo balls

ricotta blintzes with strawberry/raspberry/rhubarb sauce, topped with sour cream and sugar

truffle parmesan herbes de provence challah

almond joy unicorn challah

sun-dried tomato, pine nut, herbes de provence, parmesan challah

---

The trick was figuring out in which order to prepare these, eat everything, and be done by midnight, which is two hours past the time that my internal battery clock burns out, and I turn back into a pumpkin! Shari, you cannot afford to mess this up! The Thompsons are DSA royalty. Game on!

falafel

box of Knorr or Osem falafel mix

Add water.

Form little balls.

Fry in oil.

Open pita bread.

Spoon in hummus.

Add chopped tomato, shredded lettuce, the Israeli pickles, place in fried balls, cover with hummus. Done. Well, that was easy.

While they were enjoying their first course, I would teach them the art of chicken soup. Making falafel was bittersweet. It's a dish that Arnon made for me from scratch many times. A few months before he died, Arnon came to my house with his magical falafel balls, pita bread, homemade hummus, and his charming personality. I remember him taking my face in his hands and kissing me on each cheek that day. Arnon had no trouble showing affection, and I always felt his love and friendship, especially when he cooked for me. G-d, I miss him.

chicken soup

chopped garlic

olive oil

whole chicken

celery

oh boise!

carrots

onion

dill

parsley

turnip root

parsnip

salt

pepper

2 32-ounce boxes of chicken broth

1 packet of Manischewitz chicken soup mix

Put chopped garlic in a large pot with olive oil. Once you smell the garlic, add in four thirty-two-ounce boxes of chicken broth. Toss in the entire chicken. Okay, more like gently place the chicken into the pot. Don't make the mistake I sometimes do. Remember to remove that waxy paper baggie of chicken organs that is shoved high up into the chicken's ribs so that you have to put your entire hand inside a raw chicken carcass to dig it out. It is gross taking the bag out, but even more disgusting if you leave it in while cooking.

Add in the following peeled vegetables: turnip root, parsnip, a bunch of cut, cleaned celery, and a huge handful of carrots. Use real carrots and not those fake thumb-sized baby ones, which I do not think are really carrots. Nothing comes out of the earth looking like that. And they get all slimy after a few days in the refrigerator. They scare me.

What psycho invented those? Are we so lazy that we cannot peel and slice carrots and have resorted to these dwarf nubs?

Then put in a bunch of dill and a bunch of parsley. You can use Italian or curly, but for G-d's sake, do NOT mistake cilantro for parsley. First, the soup will taste as if it were made in Puerto Vallarta, and second, you might have some friend with that weird genetic cilantro disorder who will tell you it tastes like soap. Caryn tells me it tastes like poison. No one wants to eat something that tastes like either of those items, and it is not at all ladylike or gentlemanly to spit out chicken soup at the dinner table.

I rinse the parsley and dill, but I leave the rubber band around the bunches. No, it does not make the soup taste like an old tire, and it does make it much easier to fish out the greens when the soup is done.

Last, take the soup mix packet out of a box of Manischewitz (the "w" is pronounced as a "v" for you non-chosen folks) and mix the packet into the liquid in the pot. If you need to add water to cover everything, do it. You do not want any vegetables or chicken parts sticking out of the liquid. Cover. Bring to a boil. Cook over a low flame for about an hour. You cannot overcook it, but you can undercook it. Never undercook it. Salmonella is a big party pooper—literally.

Making soup always reminds me of a funny story. Caryn and I were sailing in a penthouse suite as invited guests onboard a Crystal Cruise in Europe. We were taken on a tour of the galley by the executive Michelin-trained chef, where we were encouraged to try gourmet delicacies: caviar, foie gras, cream puffs, and lobster bisque. One of the kitchen crew was making chicken soup.

"Should I teach you how to make real Jewish chicken soup?" I asked the chef.

Caryn hoped the floor would open and swallow her. She was so embarrassed.

"It's best to double infuse the broth," I said. "You boil chicken in water for an hour. Then you remove that chicken and add in another chicken. This time you boil the chicken WITH the vegetables and seasoning. That's what makes it double infused."

Caryn was making eye contact with the chef as if to say, "Forgive her. She doesn't know what she is saying. She has no business telling a Swiss-trained chef how to cook anything. Trust me. I have had her chicken soup. Yours has got to be better. Please don't poison our food. We are really enjoying this cruise!"

The chef winked at Caryn as if to say, "It's okay. Let her have her fun!"

Back to our recipe. While the soup is simmering, throw together the matzo meal mix. Use my grandfather's secret recipe, and you will have balls that float and not the ones your grandmother's friend used to make that needed to be cut with a knife and tasted like hockey pucks.

matzo balls

Manischewitz matzo ball mix

matzo meal

club soda

4 eggs

vegetable oil

In a medium-sized bowl, put one cup of matzo meal. Start with that second packet inside the Manischewitz soup mix—the one that is mostly matzo meal and a little seasoning. Add in enough matzo meal to make one full cup.

In another bowl, put four beaten eggs, four tablespoons of oil, and the magic ingredient: four sprays of seltzer. What is a spray of seltzer? Remember, it is my grandfather's recipe. In his day, seltzer came in glass bottles with a metal sprayer on top. I think the only reason for this was to make that iconic New York egg-cream drink that contains neither egg nor cream. It is basically chocolate milk with foam. To get the foam, you must spray the seltzer into the milk. It sounds disgusting, but when made the right way, it is nostalgic Jewish magic!

My poppy Hy's matzo ball secret is in the seltzer. I think he brought it with him from Kiev. Not the seltzer. The secret! Back in the old country, one used chicken schmaltz (fat) instead of oil. Why? Because why should Jewish food be healthy? Have you seen what we eat at our holiday meals? Chopped chicken liver, brisket, potatoes, challah, *tzimes* (tz-ih-miss), *borscht* with sour cream, *kishka* (stuffed derma), *kasha varnishkes* (bowties and buckwheat)—everything laden with grease! Oh, and cheese-stuffed blintzes. I like Eastern European Jewish food. As a kid I got used to eating tongue and *gefilte* fish. The one thing I just cannot get past my lips? Pickled herring in cream sauce with onions. Totally vile! I know many like it. I just cannot do it. Want to tell me our friendship is over? Serve me that, with a side of liver and onions for dinner. You will get rid of me quickly. Promise!

Add the liquid to the matzo meal and FOLD until absorbed. It should be somewhat loose.

You will look at it and mutter, "How am I going to make balls out of this slop?" Do not worry. You will. Put the mixture into the refrigerator for thirty minutes.

You will notice that the matzo ball batter will have slightly hardened. The key to floating, melt-in-your-mouth balls is the consistency of the batter. And the seltzer. Put a large pot of water on the stove. Add salt and boil. Form small balls from the batter that barely hold together. You want them loose, but not too loose. You are not trying to make meatballs. Drop them, one at a time, into the boiling water. Reduce the heat so that you have a very low boil; otherwise, the matzo balls will come apart. Cook for thirty minutes.

Back to the soup. Once the soup is cooked, remove the vegetables and chicken. Strain the liquid back into the pot, removing any particles. Lift the matzo balls from the hot water with a slotted spoon and place them into the soup. Let sit until you are ready to enjoy. You want the balls to absorb the flavor of the soup.

Add the carrots back. You can either slice them or puree them and mix them into the broth. If you like any of the other vegetables in your soup, add them back. I do not. I toss them. Then I let the chicken cool. I remove the skin and bones and discard. Then I cut up bite-sized pieces of chicken and add them to the soup. Delicious. Jewish penicillin.

It's time to make challah!

---

challah

5 cups of bread flour (yes, it must be bread flour). Do not ask why. I don't know. Because I am the mom.

2 eggs

6 tbsp oil (it can be any vegetable oil, including olive oil, coconut oil, herbed oil, whatever you like)

½ cup of sugar divided in half

1 tbsp and ¾ tsp of fast-acting yeast (make sure it is fresh)

1 ½ tsp salt

1 ½ cups very warm, but not hot water

In a small bowl, put one-quarter cup of sugar, yeast, and one and a half cups of very warm water. Stir and let sit a few minutes until it gets foamy. You will smell the yeast being activated.

In a large bowl, put five cups of bread flour, one-quarter cup of sugar, and the salt. Stir and combine.

In a small bowl, put two beaten eggs and the oil.

Once the yeast mixture gets foamy, add in the egg and oil mixture. Then add that mixture to the dry ingredients. Stir until you can see that you must use your hands to combine. If the dough is too sticky, add in some more flour. Once combined, form a big doughy ball and cover with a clean hand towel. Let sit until it rises (proofs) to double its size. That could take anywhere from thirty to ninety minutes. You will know when it is done. For faster results, proof in a 100 degrees oven.

Once it has risen, take the dough out of the bowl and put it on a floured surface. Knead slightly until it is no longer sticky. You may still need to sprinkle in a little more flour. Divide into three equal pieces. Now you have a decision to make. Are you going to color it?

Want to mix in some flavors and other items? You can do that before or after the dough rises. Don't overload the challah or the dough will be too heavy. Here are some of my favorites:

Almond Joy Unicorn: shredded sweetened coconut, mini chocolate chips, Oreo cookie or graham cracker cereal, and mini marshmallows if you like.

Red Head: sun-dried tomato, pine nuts, herbes de Provence, shredded parmesan cheese, and red food coloring.

Acceptance: food coloring: purple (red plus blue for those who missed the color lesson in kindergarten), blue, and green. Add gel food coloring to each ball and keep kneading until you get the color you want. You want the colors to be solid and completely overtaking the previously white dough. Both make the prettiest French toast you have ever seen! Serve with berry compote, and it is a rainbow explosion.

To Tie Dye For: same process as Acceptance, but do not continue to knead to get a solid color. You want it to look streaked.

Cin-nutty Raisin: cinnamon, brown sugar, raisins, chopped pecans.

CranApple: dried cranberries, dried apples, brown sugar.

Pesto: pine nuts, dried basil, parmesan cheese.

Scallywag: dried cranberries, shredded coconut, sweet mini chocolate chips.

Truffle Nutty Sophie: Roasted sunflower seeds, chopped pecans, herbes de Provence. Replace vegetable oil with truffle oil. Replace salt with truffle salt.

Desert Delight: dried figs, dates and apricots, raisins, cinnamon, brown sugar, slivered almonds, and coconut oil (in lieu of vegetable oil). Sprinkle with sweetened shredded coconut. Bake on a lower rack, or the coconut will burn.

Tuscan Sun: sunflower seeds, pine nuts, herbes de Provence, rosemary, parmesan cheese, truffle salt (in lieu of salt), and truffle oil (in lieu of vegetable oil).

Hawaiian crunch: diced dried pineapple, sweetened shredded coconut, and macadamia nuts (add milk chocolate chips if desired), coconut oil (in lieu of vegetable oil).

Italian Kiss: pine nuts, diced sun-dried tomatoes, minced olives, fresh oregano, shredded parmesan cheese. Sprinkle on sesame seeds after the egg wash.

BLT: crumbled crispy bacon, sun-dried tomatoes, minced chives, and herbed olive oil (in lieu of vegetable oil).

Are You Nuts?: crushed pistachio nuts, crushed pecans, sunflower seeds, crushed pumpkin seeds, sweetened shredded coconut, and any nut-flavored olive oil (in lieu of vegetable oil).

Black Forest: chopped dried cherries, sweet chocolate chips, chopped pecans, coconut oil (in lieu of vegetable oil). Sprinkle on shredded sweet coconut after the egg wash. Bake on a lower rack, or the coconut will burn.

You can add lemon or orange zest provided you dry them out. Never add in a wet ingredient. You will kill the bread. Anything dry goes. Be creative and come up with your own!

Make three equally sized balls of dough. Roll them into long strands and braid the challah. A traditional Shabbat challah has twelve humps, signifying the twelve tribes of Israel. Only a rabbi will count! A high-holiday challah is round. Same process as above, but after the braid is done, you twist it around to create a round bread. Be sure to tuck the ends under so that the bread stays intact. Gently place on a cookie sheet. Make sure you have either parchment paper or Pam, or your challah will stick.

Cover and let rise for another fifteen minutes. Wash the challah with a well-beaten egg. Top with poppy seeds, sesame seeds, or my favorite: Everything But the Bagel spice. Just do not make the mistake I did once by topping a sweet bread with the bagel seasoning. It is awful. It is like when a person toasts a cinnamon raisin bagel and adds a schmear of scallion cream cheese, smoked salmon, onion, and tomato. Why anyone would ruin smoked salmon like that, I will never know.

Each one of the Thompsons was proud of their creation.

---

blintzes

CREPE BATTER:

2 cups flour

1 cup milk

1 cup water

1 tsp salt

8 eggs

Put ingredients into a mixer and blend. Do not overmix.

FILLING:

2 cups ricotta cheese

1 tsp vanilla

¼ cup granulated sugar

1 tsp melted butter

1 egg yolk

Let the batter rest for thirty minutes. Find a six or eight inch Teflon frying pan. Go on YouTube and watch someone make crepes. Make the pancakes as thin as possible without ripping them. When cooked, they should be a little rubbery. That is what makes it easy to fold them.

Once your crepes are made, you can fill them. The key is to add just enough filling so that you get a nicely puffed-out blintz, but not so much that the cheese mixture is oozing out. The folding is critical. Place a few teaspoons of the cheese mixture in the center. Fold up from the top, covering the cheese. Then fold over from left to right and roll up to close. Place the blintzes seam-side down onto wax paper. Keep going until all the batter and filling are depleted.

Once your blintzes are assembled, fry in a larger pan with lots of unsalted butter. Make them crispy on the outside. Five minutes on each side on a medium flame will do it. Just do not let them burn. Serve with berry compote, sour cream, and sugar. Freeze remaining blintzes with wax paper in between each one.

I think about my Grammy Esther of blessed memory. She taught me how to make blintzes when I was a kid. One bite, and it brings me back to her kitchen at the Olympus in Hallandale, Florida, where I would make blintzes and squeeze my own orange juice.

Using the electric orange juice maker with my Poppa Joe, also of blessed memory, was a Strassner grandchild rite of passage. Poppa Joe would carefully position us at the juicer, holding an orange, ready for action. He would take out his Kodak Instamatic and say, "Who loves you?"

The answer was, "Everybody!"

We all learned at a young age that THIS was the only answer.

My cousin Kenny couldn't say everybody, so he said, "Izzy Daddy." I even have a photo of my kids, who were born after my grandfather passed, in that same pose. My grandfather was a rough and tumble, no-nonsense guy. He said it as he saw it, even if we did not want to hear it. His heart was big, and he loved us very much. He just had a hard time giving a compliment. I remember in my chubby prepubescent days, I would fly down from New York to visit Grammy Esther and Poppa Joe. One time, I arrived at the airport and saw them as I exited the plane. Yes, before September 11, 2001, a passenger could be greeted AT the plane. I ran to Poppa Joe. His outstretched arms were ready to welcome me.

I said, "Hi, Poppa Joe!"

He said, "You picked up some weight there, baby!"

I learned to develop a thick skin. I was not angry with him. In my family you did not survive without a thick skin. I refused to eat for most of the vacation and went home a few pounds lighter, but I did drink lots of orange juice!

Back to baking. The challah has now risen for the second time. Put the loaves in the oven at 350 degrees for thirty to forty minutes. Challah laden with extra ingredients will take longer. Keep watching. If the outside is golden brown and you can knock on or push in the top, and if it springs back, it is probably ready. You can enjoy it hot or cooled down. Best to cool on a wire baking rack.

Our cooking and eating fest went on for hours.

It was 11:30 p.m. when Orville turned to me and said, "Let's buy a cruise!"

Fortunately, Caryn and Eldon had prepared the quotes and pricing grids so that I could explain why allowing Royal Caribbean to keep their money and roll it into a 2022 program made good business sense. I spoke for five minutes. Orville picked up his phone. He texted Dan Orchard, the company president, and his brother Chuck, who oversees the events team.

"Okay, we're all in!" Orville said.

He said YES to the same deal he had said no to ever since June. What changed? Human connection. That is what changed. It was then I remembered the saying that 90 percent of life is just showing up. I had shown up. I cared. I engaged. I gave of myself. I connected, and I shared personal details about my sexuality.

Orville put his arm around me and said, "We love you, and we accept you."

It was the first time in months that I had happy tears in my eyes.

He accepted me!

I had been hiding behind a shroud of secrecy and heterosexuality for years, afraid that clients wouldn't want to work with me if they knew I was different. I have never liked labels or boxes or fitting in. I didn't want to be judged, questioned, or rejected. I was afraid. And now I felt relieved.

"You know," Orville said, "one of our neighbors, Monica Tanner, was Jewish before she joined the church."

Monica is a self-proclaimed sex and relationship therapist.

A Mormon sex therapist?

"Monica would love this matzo ball soup!" Orville exclaimed.

Within minutes, accompanied by her daughters Sophie and Brinley, she was standing in the kitchen, tasting challah and sipping soup.

"Can you do this tomorrow night at our house? Would you have Shabbat dinner with us?" Monica asked.

Why not?

Caryn, Jaci, me, Sandy, Ana, and Robbyanne.
I thank G-d for them every day.

Ninety-five days
with this trusty
Kipling carry-on.

Leah, Logan, Livvy, Luke, and me at the bear house.

Morty Shapiro and me under the arch at Northwestern. Congrats Jake!

I turned on my smile hanging out with Mary in Minneapolis.

My big catch in Tofte! Enthralled by fishing!

Mazel Tov Joey Kerper. Here's to you!

Orville Thompson and me at his lake in Idaho.

My young student, Micah Blair (9) making tye dye challah for the first time.

A prismatic inside Yellowstone. OMG that color!

Mazel tov Alexandra and Etai.
PHOTO CREDIT: Jill Paice

"Write the book, Shari!" So I did. Thanks Ruth. You inspired me.

I can still taste the huckleberry
ice cream from Jackson Drug.

Yeah, my back and tush
hurt for a few days, but the
scenery was amazing!

Apparently, Layne doesn't like frolicking either.

These mussels will ruin you from ever ordering them in a restaurant.

Grammy Esther's blintzes are one of a kind. You'll kvell with delight.

Who knew I could kill mosquitos with a salt gun?

Kendra's FB post: Thanks @buysea for teaching me your wonderful ways of baking

Personal space Scallywag! Boundaries! He is me . . . in dog form.

My first glamping experience. My Girl Scout skills at work!

There was zero
chance I was getting
naked in that shower!

Politically incorrect Timmy and his Jewish tourist from New York.
I am sure he was thrilled!

The mug.
I had to have it.
It was a sign!

Adventure follows me wherever I go. Coral Pink Sand Dunes.

My new friend Sandy at the post office near Bryce Canyon.

Sue and me in her kitchen
in Scottsdale. One grain at a time.

At a vortex in Sedona.
I never felt peace
like this before.

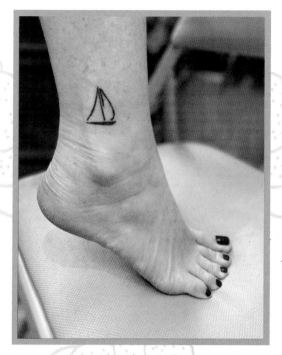

My one and only tattoo.
Yes, it hurt, but it was worth it.

Ray and the cloud eggs.
The first time one of his
guests cooked breakfast!

Michele, how do you feel about a hot air balloon ride?

I miss Grammy Esther's chopped liver, Passover apple cake, perfect coleslaw and the times she would show up with lamb chops for my freezer. Thank goodness she passed along her talent for making blintzes and those fabulous fishing skills!

She Was Enthralled By Fishing!

The following morning, I texted Monica a shopping list. We would make blintzes, challah, and matzo ball soup. I arrived at her house at 6:30 p.m.

As we started to cook, Monica said, "The Thompsons are coming over too!"

Didn't they have enough Jewish food for a lifetime? Apparently, they liked it so much, they wanted seconds. It was close to Rosh Hashanah. I had an idea. Let's celebrate the Jewish new year together. We got candles, glasses of grape juice (remember, Mormons do not drink alcohol), matzo ball soup, blintzes, and of course, challah!

Baruch atah Adonai, Eloheinu melech ha'olam, hamotzi lechem min ha'aretz. Amen. (blessing over the food)

Blessed are You, Adonai, our G-d, Sovereign of all, who brings forth bread from the earth. Amen.

Baruch atah Adonai, Eloheinu melech ha'olam, borei p'ri hagafen. (blessing over the wine/grape juice)

Blessed are you Adonai, our G-d, Ruler of the Universe, who creates the fruit of the vine. Amen.

Baruch atah Adonai, Eloheinu melech ha'olam, borei p'ri ha'eitz. (blessing over the apples and honey)

Blessed are you, Adonai, our G-d, Ruler of the Universe, Creator of the fruit of the tree. Amen.

They asked me to explain many of the Jewish traditions. Although Monica had converted before marriage, she still held onto all her grandmother's cookbooks and other Jewish paraphernalia. I think my visit brought her back to her roots. I always feel connected to Judaism when I cook traditional foods and recite the associated prayers.

Before the end of the evening, Orville asked me, "Do you want to go fishing with me?"

Fishing! I am enthralled by fishing! "I would love to!" I replied with a huge smile.

"Great, I will pick you up tomorrow at 10:00 a.m. and take you to my lake," said Orville.

A lake? He owned an entire lake? Awesome. Saturday at 10:00 a.m., accompanied by his eighty-six-year-old dad, Leon, Orville came to get me. We drove to his lake. It wasn't just a lake. It was a compound the size of Central Park with a huge body of water in the middle. Orville had built a reception center, which looks like a modern conference center, for their October family wedding. There were bountiful gardens, space to build an entire housing development, a huge garage, a few trucks, and new Kentucky Derby–style fencing of which Orville was particularly proud. I was blown away. We went into the garage to retrieve some fishing poles. Off to the lake.

"Do you REALLY know how to fish?" Orville asked me.

"Of course, I do. Are we bottom fishing or casting?" I asked.

"Casting," he replied. "Here, let me help you."

Remember, my father used to take me fishing when I was a kid. "Thanks, but I don't need help," I exclaimed.

And just like Dad taught me, I sent the line way out into the middle of the lake. BAM! I hooked a bass! I did not tell Orville I had one on the line until I had reeled it in. No one cares about those fish-that-got-away stories.

"Is this what I am supposed to catch?" I joked, holding up a nice big one.

Orville came over and removed the fish from the hook and showed me how to hold it up for a photo. A little trick: hold the fish out in front of you and it looks larger!

My next catch was the size of a sardine. Leon, Orville, and I had a good laugh. The trip was short because Orville had a golf date with his son-in-law's father. Orville told Leon about the challah we had made together two nights before.

"Will you make me a challah?" asked Leon.

Sure! I would be happy to. I sent Heidi a text asking which kind Leon would like.

"Plain," she said.

I baked Leon a stunning challah and delivered it later. He and his wife loved it!

The following day was Sunday. Once a month, the Gales attend in-person church. I had never been to a Mormon church service and decided to go along. Eldon is an accomplished pianist and has the voice of an angel. He is the only client I have ever had who loves Broadway music as much as I do. Eldon would be playing at services. I was eager to listen.

We arrived for the 10:30 a.m. service and sat alone in our pew. There were no books. There were not many families, but as you can imagine, each family had four or five children. All were perfectly dressed and well-behaved. I learned about the sacrament service, which is akin to Catholic communion, yet the bread is actual store-bought white bread, not a thin, quickly melting wafer. They should buy my challah! And the blood of Jesus is a thimbleful of tap water. The ritual of covering the bread and the water with a white cloth and the prayer that is recited is the same at every Mormon service. At this service, Max Gale, seventeen, offered the prayer. It must be done exactly as written, or the speaker must start at the beginning. Max got it on the first try.

Young church members walked around with trays and offered the bread and water to everyone. I suppose each religion has its own way of honoring G-d. In this case, Jesus Christ the prophet. Several members got up to speak. The bishop "called" and "released" members from their duties as religion teachers, youth group leaders, and church officiates.

Once the service was over, we met two missionaries outside. I learned that a female missionary is called a sister, and a male missionary is called an elder. Other than seeing *The Book of Mormon* on Broadway and having many conversations with Eldon and his family, I had never been on the inside. Well, there was that one time when Eldon suggested I visit the new Mormon temple being built in Davie, Florida. He said anyone could see it before its dedication. So, Caryn and I went. WOW! What a palace! I had never seen any building with such extraordinary construction in Florida. Every detail was perfect. I got to see the baptismal—a locker room where temple recommends can change into white garb; the sealing room—where members get married; and my personal favorite, the celestial room. The celestial room looked like the most gorgeous living room you have ever seen. It is all white. It has seats and couches and a spectacular ceiling. It is peaceful. It is perfect. All I would need is a good book and a pumpkin spice latte, and I could spend an entire day there!

I do not think I would make a good Mormon. I need caffeine and an occasional old-fashioned. Instead of saying, "Oh my word!" I might let too many expletives fly.

Shari, stick to Judaism.

At least they accepted me, even though I was an outsider. I know people who joke about the Church of Jesus Christ of Latter-day Saints. We can poke fun at all religions, I suppose. The one thing I know is that this religion celebrates family time. They enjoy being together. They are upbeat and warm. As far as I could see on my trip to Boise, I was welcome, and I was not judged even though my beliefs differed from theirs. It felt wonderful, and I gained so much respect. I will not be converting, but I will forever appreciate their way of life.

chapter nine

where the deer and the antelope play

I had planned to drive or fly to Coeur d'Alene, Idaho, after leaving Boise, but the fires had gotten out of control, and there was a lot of smoke in northwestern Idaho and eastern Washington. Sadly, I had to cancel my stop.

"Where should I go instead?" I asked Eldon.

"Have you ever been to Jackson Hole, the Grand Tetons, or Yellowstone?" he questioned.

NO! On this trip I had ticked off Idaho and Mississippi. I still had a list of states to which I had never been: Wyoming, New Mexico, Montana, West Virginia, Kansas, Nebraska, Arkansas, North Dakota, South Dakota.

Eldon said, "Stay at the Antler Inn. It's right in town. It's not fancy, but it's perfect. Book some tours and enjoy. Make sure you take 'the money shot' in front of the elk antler arches and have a drink at the Million Dollar Cowboy Bar."

Okay, why not? "Do I fly there?" I wondered.

"You could, but the part of the drive from Idaho Falls to Jackson is stunning. You should drive!" encouraged Eldon. "I will drop you off at the Boise Airport to get a car. On the way, you can visit the new Scentsy headquarters,"

Awesome. I was excited to embrace it all. On Monday, September 13, I had my last heavenly massage with Carmen. And then, Eldon and I headed to Scentsy. It is a spectacular, state-of-the-art campus of buildings that includes a wax factory. The wax is made there, and Orville prides himself on employing as many Americans as possible. As it was explained to me, the warmers are made in China, which is why the material is called china. The Chinese have perfected the product. Additionally, manufacturing in China keeps the product costs down, and makes the purchase affordable in the United States to a wide audience.

In the lobby of the offices were displays that included newly released warmers and waxes, the original Crock-Pot that Orville had started with back in 2003, the inaugural warmers, and other Scentsy memorabilia. I think Eldon was proudest of the dozens of licensed Disney products.

He brought me over to one corner and said, "This is the line that makes us the most money, *The Nightmare Before Christmas,* the movie that inspired the name of the line. This is one of the reasons why we are having our best year ever!"

I had Eldon take photos of everything I wanted to send to my Florida and New York homes. I HAD to have more Scentsy in my life!

After the tour, I picked up a Kia Sorrento at the Boise Airport and headed for Jackson Hole, the longest drive I would be doing thus far. Three hundred and sixty-nine miles. I was a little anxious about doing this drive alone, but I was up for the challenge. I remember Eldon telling me that the Boise to Idaho Falls part is barren wasteland, dry and ugly. Only after that, it is lovely. He wasn't kidding. Nothing to look at but big brown hills for miles and hours.

About twenty minutes outside of Idaho Falls, I decided to refuel and use the restroom. As I exited the freeway, I heard scraping underneath the car. I pulled into the gas station and had to lie down next to the car to look underneath. I am no car expert like my brother, Jay, who owns a few dozen Jiffy Lubes in New Jersey. Would I know if something was wrong? If so, what the hell could I do about it? There it was. Some unspecified black thing hanging lower than it should have been. Great. Now what? First, I had to pee. Second, I needed gas.

And then I called Hertz Roadside Assistance. "Hello? I am driving one of your cars from Boise to Jackson Hole. There seems to be a problem, and I need someone to come and help me," I calmly requested.

"Where are you?" asked the operator.

"I don't exactly know, but I took the exit that said I was twenty miles from Idaho City. Does that help?" I asked.

"Can you hold on, please?" he requested.

Sure. Did I have another option? I sat on hold for seventeen minutes before he came back. I know it was seventeen minutes because I took a screenshot if I had to prove my case later and get money off the bill, which I promise you, I would.

"Hi. Is the car drivable?" he asked.

"I drove it this far. I guess so. But there is this scraping sound, and the black cover thing is hanging too low. Is there a Hertz in Idaho Falls where I can swap it for another vehicle?" I asked.

"No, we don't have one in Idaho Falls," he said.

I thought that was weird. Isn't there an airport there? But I did not question him.

"So, what am I supposed to do? I must get to Jackson Hole before dark. I am alone. I have no sense of direction. Can someone come and help me?" I asked.

"I suggest you just drive it to Jackson Hole. Since you only have the car for one day, return it to the airport there," he said.

What happens if I drive this car, the black thing drags along the road, ignites, and the car blows up? I will die in a fiery crash before I ever get to see Yellowstone. That would suck. Then someone must identify my charred body and call my kids. Then my kids will tell people that their mother had gone on a cross-country journey during COVID while everyone else is staying home quarantining. No one knows the combination to the safe in my house or where I keep the keys to the safety deposit box at the bank, which I call the vault because that is what my grandmother called it. And what about the FSU class I am teaching on Wednesday? Shelly Griffin will wonder what happened to me.

Every Jew can go from zero to worst-possible scenario in five minutes or less. Fine! I would drive the car. It was clear no one was coming to rescue me. And this could be good for $50 off the rental. Who doesn't love a discount?

I hesitantly got back on the road. The scraping sound continued and worsened. I felt uneasy. I heard a POP! My entire body tensed up. I quickly checked the rear-view mirror. Flying behind the car was the black piece that had become detached from the chassis and was now airborne. I had to look ahead through the windshield to drive, so I could not see if it had landed on another car or on the road. Regardless, there was nothing I could do. I hoped no one got hurt. At least the scraping sound was gone. I drove another two hours, waiting for more car parts to spontaneously fly off of the vehicle. Thank G-d they never did!

Tired, with my nerves a bit fried, I arrived at the Jackson Hole Airport, which they should just call the Jackson Hole Air Strip. If you sneeze, you miss it. I parked the car. I noted the mileage. I figured someone would ask. I had prepurchased the fuel and was returning the car as close to empty as possible. I got to the counter. Surely the representative would understand my story and either comp the rental or give me a discount for my trouble. No such luck.

"This is a Boise car. You have to call Boise if you want a resolution," she said. "Here, fill out this form."

I wrote down what happened and was fearful that I would be responsible for damage. I never take out the supplemental car insurance. My father always told me it is a big waste of money. Hertz might think that I had run over something that caused the black thing to hang low, and then I would get charged for having it ripped off the vehicle. Whatever. I was in Jackson Hole, Wyoming. THE Jackson Hole, Wyoming. Now I had to get from the airport to the Antler Inn. There was no Uber or Lyft. There was one SUV waiting outside.

When the driver saw me emerge, he approached. "Do you need a taxi?" he asked

Yes! I did need a taxi. It was $40 to go ten minutes down the road. Forty dollars? That sounded like a lot, but this was the only taxi, so I guess I had no choice. I got in. The driver saw another passenger, an elderly man, looking for a ride. He asked if I would be willing to share and split the fare with this traveler. I was!

The man entered the vehicle. He was going to the Antler Inn too! What luck! Twenty dollars was better than $40. Turned out the man comes to town two times a year to visit the grave of his wife, who is buried near the Tetons. They used to vacation in Jackson Hole often, and her dying wish was to make this her final resting place. The man told me that her ashes are buried here. He comes to talk to her. For the amount it cost to come from Lubbock to Jackson Hole, I hope she answers him.

We arrived at the Antler Inn, and the driver asked each of us for $30. Thirty dollars? The cab ride should have been $40 regardless of the number of people. I am not a math whiz, but that would be $20 each. Right?

"No," said the driver. "When you share, each person pays $30."

WHAT? So, if three of us shared, the driver would have collected $90 for a $40 ride?

I did not have the energy to argue, and I did not want to embarrass myself in front of this other passenger, who reminded me of the elderly man from Disney's *UP*. I paid the $30 and exited the car. I hope he was not also expecting a gratuity.

The Antler Inn did not disappoint. It was perfect. No Ritz Carlton, but it was authentic and charming. There was free coffee in the lobby and a laundromat in the basement.

I had a moment and checked my text messages. This one from Eldon truly brightened my day:

FYI, Heidi and Orville are on a call right now with all of Scentsy's top consultants. They just referenced their friend who came to town who thinks differently from them, believes, lives, and worships differently from them, but we could still come together, cook together, and have a wonderful time learning from each other.

I replied, "I love that!"

Eldon continued, "The world just needs more Jews and Mormons having dinner together."

I agree. The world needs more people connecting with other people, especially those who are different from themselves. Amen. Thank you, lucky star. You really came through for me.

I walked around town. It was like something out of a fairy tale, forty-nin-er-er style. There were shops, restaurants, and a lot of charm. There was no diversity to be found. Not a single person of color, nor a same-sex couple holding hands. Just lots of straight white people with money to burn. And MAGA hats everywhere. Many of the stores in Jackson were selling MAGA shirts, hats, bumper stickers, and other right-leaning paraphernalia. I found a wonderful red, velvety-soft zip-up jumpsuit with moose all over it that I had to have for my friend Krista's baby, Layne.

As I reached to take it down from the rack, I brushed up against a deliciously soft, long-sleeved blue T-shirt with Jackson Hole emblazoned on the front, back, and sleeves. I must have this for Krista. I grabbed both items and went to the register. There, next to the machine, sat a stuffed moose wearing a TRUMP 2020 hat and a bear wearing a Biden/Harris cap. More politics! I wanted to leave, but I wanted the items more. As the cashier was ringing up the purchases, I turned the moose and the bear to face the other way. I expressed my unhappiness to the Romanian cashier. Was there anywhere to escape the presidential race? I just wanted to shop in peace.

She said, "I agree with you, but I need this job."

On my walk, I passed a hand-dipped candle store. There was one young girl crafting a skull out of wax. I looked around the shop. These candles were stunning. The colors were fun, cheerful, and multilayered. I wanted one. I wanted two. I wanted all of them.

The girl explained, "If you buy four, you get one free."

Free? Did she say free? I love free. Free is good.

Okay. I started to collect these fabulous round, glossy candles and placed them on the shelf in front of the girl. Five, six, seven. Oh no! I had seven I liked. Now I had to buy eight to get two free. Okay. Eight, nine, ten. There! Ten candles. I would send them to the girls at Buy the Sea, one for each of my kids, one for Teva, one for Krista, and a few left over.

The girl requested, "Can I take a photo? My coworker who made these candles yesterday is never going to believe this!"

"Of course," I replied.

I FaceTimed Caryn: show me which one you want and which you think the girls will like so that I can label the boxes.

Now I had to figure out how to ship them home. When I got to my hotel room, I unpacked the candles. WAIT! There weren't ten candles. There were eleven! I don't know if it was a mistake or a gift, but never look a gift horse in the mouth.

WHAT? Who coined that phrase? If you get a horse as a gift and you look him in the mouth, are you cursed for all eternity?

I had dinner at a small Japanese restaurant called SUDA. I sat alone at the bar. It was the first time I had been alone in a restaurant since the start of my journey. I am not a fan of eating in a public place by myself. I feel everyone is looking at me, thinking, *Poor girl. Couldn't get a date?* So, I decided to get chatty with the waitress. I asked her what I should NOT leave the restaurant without trying.

"Definitely the scallops and the salmon sashimi with truffle ponzu sauce," she said.

She had me at truffle. I had a saketini too. After nine days with Mormons, it was time to have an adult beverage. It was awesome, and so was the food. On my way back to the Antler Inn, I passed Jackson Drug. This is anything BUT a drugstore. It is an old-fashioned malt shop.

On the menu? Huckleberry ice cream. Step away from this place. Run, don't walk. But I had to have some, and I had to have some right now! During COVID, you must order at the front with the hostess. Or you can sit at a table outside, and a waiter will take your order and bring the food.

I approached the hostess, another Romanian—I could detect the accent at this point.

"What can I get for you?" she asked.

"I would like one scoop of huckleberry ice cream with chocolate sprinkles," I replied.

A young man behind the counter started to assemble my sugar cone with one scoop. He dipped it into the sprinkles and handed it to me before I even had a chance to pay. So here I am, HOLDING what I ordered.

The girl said, "$5.36, please."

Okay. I pulled out my credit card while balancing the cone in the other hand. Ice cream now paid for and received.

"What is your name?" the girl asked.

"Shari," I replied.

"How do you spell that?" she asked.

"S-H-A-R-I," I answered.

"That is a weird way to spell it," she said.

"A weird way to spell what?" I questioned.

"Sherry. That is a weird way to spell Sherry," she added.

"Well, if my name WERE Sherry, then yes, it would be a weird way to spell Sherry. But my name is Shari. The 'a' is pronounced like apple. And why do you need my name?" I wondered.

"So that we can find you to deliver the ice cream," she explained.

"You mean the ice cream that is in my hands?" I asked.

Puzzled stare (her). No comment (me). I left Jackson Drug and walked back to the motel. Time to go to bed, but first I called the Boise Hertz location to advise them of—aka complain about—my experience with their car.

"Hello, sir. This is Shari Wallack. I rented one of your vehicles and had some issues," I told him.

"Oh yes, I was planning to call you. I am so sorry to hear about your struggles with our car and especially roadside assistance. I'd like to take $50 off your rental to make up for your time and aggravation," he offered.

Now THAT would never happen in New York. Idahoans sure are nice!

On Tuesday, September 15, I was set to go on a full-day tour of Yellowstone. I was dressed, ready, and excited when the van from Yellowstone Tours pulled up. I was the last one to be collected. There were four couples and me, plus Pete, the driver.

"You can sit in the front next to me since you are the only one traveling alone," said Pete.

Was I being shamed already for vacationing solo? I did not care. I was so happy to finally see Yellowstone. We passed the Grand Tetons and headed an hour north. I am a morning person, and I realize that not everyone else shares my 7:00 a.m. enthusiasm, so I was quiet most of the way.

Yellowstone was stunning. I saw geothermic miracles I had seen before only in *National Geographic*. Was this real? Was I actually looking at this? The yellow stones—hence the name—were golden and sparkling in the sun. I know you are not supposed to take anything from a national park, but those stones! What if I could find some just outside the park? That wasn't illegal. I had to have some as proof that I had seen this force of nature in person.

While others in the group were waiting for Old Faithful to erupt, our driver, Pete, took me to a safe place. I started to gather a handful of stones, not as vibrant as the ones in the park, but still yellow, and some sticks that had fallen from the trees. The trees are so unique in this part of the country, and the dead limbs fascinated me. Yellowstone is known for having swarms of bark beetles that attack the trees, making interesting grooves and patterns. It looks as if a skilled woodworker has carved the designs into the bark. I had to have some of those as well.

I took what I could and put them into my small bag. The nature chains! The ones Dan had in his house. I wanted a nature chain. It would be the best souvenir! I had to mail these items to him. I was traveling with a small carry-on bag, and I certainly was not going to weigh it down with dirty rocks and twigs.

"Pete," I asked. "Is there a post office in the park? Can you take me there? I want to send a mug to a friend of mine in Minneapolis."

"Where is the mug?" Pete asked.

"I have not bought it yet," I replied.

Pete took me back inside the park to the gift shop. I found a mug for Dan. Perfect. Maybe it would be his next Sunday morning Facebook mug post! We went to the post office. It was the tiniest post office I had ever seen. No lobby. One small table to pack a box.

"Excuse me, sir, can I have that shoe-box-sized Priority Mail box behind you? And do you have tape and bubble wrap?" I requested.

"I can give you the box, but we don't have bubble wrap, and I have to tape the box for you," he said.

Oh shit! No bubble wrap. What if the mug breaks? How do I keep the sticks and stones from rattling around? I have got to get this to Dan.

I formed the box and held the bottom together with my hands.

I put in the rocks, the sticks, and last, the mug that had been wrapped a few times in paper at the store. I labeled the box and handed it to the clerk to tape.

As he turned it upside down to tape the other side, he heard the rumbling. "Can you tell me what is inside this box making all that noise?" he asked.

SHIT! I am going to prison for taking rocks and dead sticks from outside the park! How would he know where I collected them? Why didn't I just go to the post office in downtown Jackson Hole? What was I thinking?

"Sure, it's toys!" I exclaimed.

Toys, Shari? Seriously? What kind of toy makes those noises?

"What kind of toys?" he asked.

HOLY HELL! UGH . . . kids' toys.

"My kids and I are traveling, and I need to send their toys home because they don't fit in the suitcase with all the souvenirs we bought. It's marbles and matchbox cars," I said.

Did that just come out of my mouth? I am screwed. He is going to open the box and see that I am lying, or he is going to ask to meet my kids, who are twenty-two and twenty-four years old. They are not likely to play with marbles and cars, and besides, they are not even with me. STAY CALM. Do not let him see you sweat.

"Okay, I just need to put my seal on the box so that no one questions the rattling," he told me.

WHAT? He just bought my story? He could not possibly be that naive. Thank G-d he was.

I spent the next few hours wondering if the box would make it to Dan.

I kept imagining the Minneapolis police knocking on Dan's door, box in hand. "Do you know the whereabouts of Shari Wallack? You are both under arrest for conspiring to deplete Yellowstone of its natural resources."

And if that didn't happen and the box actually did make it to Dan, would I have bad luck like the time Peter Brady stole the idol from the volcano in Hawaii and all kinds of crazy shit started happening to him and the rest of the Bunch? I was doomed.

We left the post office and got to Old Faithful within moments of its scheduled eruption. We collected the other tour passengers and drove back to Jackson Hole. What an incredible excursion!

Wednesday, September 16, was a magical day. It was the day I was to teach those two sessions at Florida State University, and the day that Etai, and his gorgeous bride Alexandra, were to be married in Central Park. It was not the wedding they had envisioned, surrounded by more than a hundred friends and family, but one that they had spontaneously planned because they could not wait for COVID to disappear before saying I do.

7:05 a.m. The students at FSU were waiting for me on Zoom.

Be memorable, Shari. Stick to the topics. Cram it all into fifty minutes.

Memorable? Of course. Clad in my Snoopy Halloween pajamas, I greeted the class. I shared with them a few of my philosophies on entrepreneurship. Figure out what your brand is. What makes you unique? Find it and stick with it. The most important thing about branding is to be authentic. Be authentically YOU. Does that mean YOU can wear Snoopy pajamas to a presentation? Probably not.

I engaged with the class until Shelly told me it was quitting time. I loved every single minute.

One of the kids asked me, "Do you wake up like this every morning? And if you drink something to get this kind of energy, would you mind sharing what it is?"

I laughed. Yup, this was me! No caffeine. Full-on Shari. I explained that I do wake up this way, and I am pretty much like this until about 9:00 p.m. when my battery runs down. Then I sleep like a baby for about ten hours!

At the 1:25 p.m. session, I was even more awake and eager. After that session ended, we engaged in a ninety-minute Q&A. I had more time to give some specific advice on entrepreneurship and what I think makes someone successful, regardless of the industry. I agreed to mentor, for free, any student who wanted help and to work with Shelly on the students' final projects later in the year.

I have never wanted to be a teacher, but I think it is selfish to have had so many experiences and success and not share it with future business mavens.

Later that day, I approached my alma mater, Adelphi University. They had signed me up to speak to their business school students and be a judge at their year-end entrepreneurship contest. Score!

By the evening, my phone had blown up with some lovely photos of the wedding. Alexandra looked stunning in a lacy white dress, bright blue shoes, and the most beautiful smile. Etai looked like the sophisticated man Arnon would have been proud to have raised. Etai was glowing with joy. I sent him a text that read:

Dearest Etai,

Remember on April 17, when you said to me through red, swollen, and teary eyes that you could not imagine ever being happy again? I can see in the photos how very happy you are. Abba would be delighted. Mazel tov, my dear friend. I am so very happy for you and Alexandra.

With love, Shari

September 17, and I was off to the Grand Tetons. Sadly, the smoke from the West Coast fires clouded our view, yet it was still spectacular. We started at Mormon Row, a location of early settlers. They had found land and had built their houses in a row to live in a close-knit community. Many of the houses still stand.

I could not stop snapping photos. It was so picturesque. Each house was unique and completely intact. The colors were vibrant, and the Tetons in the distance made for the most majestic backdrop. We then drove around the park, searching for animals. Bison, elk, deer. It was stunning and fun to watch animals in their natural habitat and not behind a cage or in a theme park. One of the highlights was to be a one-hour tour by boat of Jenny Lake. COVID canceled the lake tours, yet we could still take a boat over to the other side of the park for a short hike to a waterfall.

I asked our guide Josh, "Is this a hike or a walk? Is it uphill? I am wearing sandals, and I don't have a walking stick."

"It's mostly flat," he replied.

Great! I love a nice walk.

Josh's idea of flat was not the same as mine. It was ALL uphill and rocky. I did not know if I could make it, but I pushed myself. There at the top was the most beautiful cascade. I could not help but think that G-d made this, and I should thank Him. I looked at the water and sang:

Shema Yisrael. Adonai eloheynu. Adonai Echad.

The Lord is our G-d. The Lord is one.

I am not religious, but it felt like the right thing to do.

When I was done chanting, I walked back to the boat launch. There stood a family of Amish people.

Oh boy! I am going to meet them!

"Hello. You are Amish, right?" I asked.

"Yes," said the grandfatherly looking elder.

"I have never met anyone Amish, and I would love to speak with you and learn about your family," I said. "Would that be okay?"

"Sure," said the man. "My name is Dan. This is my wife and five of our eleven children."

ELEVEN?

His wife reminded me of this eighty-six-year-old Czech woman, Anna Comicek, who cleaned our house when I was a kid.

"Wow, that's wonderful," I said. "Where do you live?" I asked him.

"Wisconsin, near Madison," he said.

"I thought you weren't able to ride in an actual car. I thought you get around only by horse and buggy," I questioned. "How did you get here?"

"We had a driver take us from Wisconsin to Wyoming," he replied.

They were all dressed in typical Amish attire. The mom and daughters were clad in drab solid-colored dresses with pins attaching one side to the other. Buttons are too fancy, I was told. The boys looked like Charles Ingalls on *Little House on the Prairie*. I continued to ask questions.

"What do you do for a living?" I wanted to know.

"We are farmers, and we make furniture," Dan explained.

I asked them about shunning, birth control, rumspringa, *Breaking Amish,* and shoefly pie. I asked them how they got their news if they did not use any technology. No TV, movies, cell phones, computers.

Dan said, "We don't get news unless it is from our own community."

No news?

No continuous loop of political commentary, coronavirus, the stock market, Russia, China, North Korea? NO NEWS! And then it hit me. They seemed so kind, peaceful, calm. No anxiety. Why in the world would they have anxiety? Their world was filled with baking, sewing, farming, church, singing family songs, and making babies. There was no competition. No makeup or hair dye or mani/pedis. No show tunes! I asked Dan if he was happy.

"Yes, of course I am happy. G-d has taken good care of my family and me," he said.

I thanked him for speaking with me. I was sad that we could not take a photo, as the Amish do not pose for pictures. I wondered how old Dan and his wife were. *Seventy-five? Eighty?* I could not tell. So, I asked.

"Would you be insulted if I asked you how old you are?"

"We are both fifty-eight," he answered.

NO WAY! Fifty-eight! I am almost fifty-seven, and I look as if I could be their granddaughter.

I tried to wipe away the expression of utter shock. "You look wonderful," I said.

And I meant it. Yes, they appeared elderly with their white hair, but they seemed genuinely happy. There is much to be said about happiness. Perhaps finding true inner peace is to follow Marie Kondo's advice: Get rid of those items that do not bring you joy. Declutter your life. Relationships, not things, are the most critical, starting with your most important relationship, the one you have with yourself.

I was slowly giving up my need to be the best: RCCL's Account of the Year, the industry superstar. The accolades were no longer there to fill my bucket. The money I had saved was now giving me freedom to figure out who I could be without Buy the Sea. I knew at that moment that I had to do something more than sell cruises for the next thirty years of my life. And how was I going to make a difference in the world? I was hoping to find out.

The following day I was scheduled to pick up a car and drive to Salt Lake City. I woke up and walked to the only car rental place in town. I had wheels again! As I was driving back to the Antler Inn, my phone rang. It was Ruth Levine Schmid. I had met Ruth many years ago at a trade show where we were possibly the only two Jews in attendance. We have remained friends ever since. She founded a professional speakers bureau and was now semiretired and loving life in San Diego with her husband John. Their elder son had recently graduated from Harvard, and the other was finishing up at Columbia.

Mama didn't raise no dummies! Before the fires started, I had been planning to go to southern California after Coeur d'Alene, but my trip had taken a different turn. I would tackle California later.

"Shari, are you here?" she asked me.

"No, I didn't end up going to San Diego," I told her. "I am in Jackson Hole!"

"Yes, I know. I saw you on Facebook. I am in Jackson Hole too! I am spending the fall here. When can we get together?" she asked.

"I am going horseback riding at 1:30 p.m., and then I am driving to Salt Lake," I told her.

"Can we meet before you leave?" she asked.

"Absolutely," I said. "How about lunch at Jackson Drug?"

Perfect. I had a lot to do before meeting Ruth at 11:00 a.m. I had to pack up my things and find a post office to ship home those candles and some sweatshirts I had bought in the Tetons.

Ruth met me at the hotel, and we walked to Jackson Drug. I was so excited to see a friend in this mountain paradise. We ordered soup. And of course, I had another helping of huckleberry ice cream, which was my motive for picking that location. Over lunch I told her about all my adventures.

"Only you would make lemonade out of lemons, Shari. Actually, you are making limoncello!" she said. "You should write a book! And then you can go on the speakers' circuit and talk about it," she said.

A book? I do not know how to write a book. But maybe I should?

"I know! I will call it Flour Power!" I said.

"No," said Ruth. "That sounds like a seventies hippie cookbook. Call it something else."

"What do you think of *from hell to challah*?" I asked her.

"PERFECT. I love that," she exclaimed. "I will do some research for you on how to get some representation and speaking engagements. But first you need to publish the book."

Okay, I would find time to write the book!

chapter ten

g-d bless kurt

Although it was not in my original plan, I was off to Lehi, a suburb of Salt Lake City, to visit Krista, her husband Kurt, and one-year-old Layne Jackson. Krista is a former client. She worked for a company called Tahitian Noni, which later became Morinda and was subsequently purchased by NewAge.

Salt Lake City is the direct-selling mecca. Companies like Nuskin, Usana, Young Living Essential Oils, and a whole host of others with unusual names such as Xango and Xyngular are based there. Take the Mormon recruiting model, add some products that are guaranteed to cure every imaginable disease or make your skin look younger than a baby's, give it a unique name no one can spell, and you have quite a remarkable yet often-scrutinized industry.

I had met Krista in person when she and Kurt sailed with me on the *Crystal Esprit* yacht. We cruised around the Grenadines together. I had invited other clients too. On the first night I got everyone together and introduced them to each other. We played a fun word association game so that we would all remember each other's names. When I got to Kurt, I called him G-d Bless Kurt, like when Maria could not remember one child's name during the rainstorm scene in *The Sound of Music*. Ever since, I call him G-d Bless Kurt, and I hear it has stuck with some of their family members!

The Jacksons are members of the church, but not as observant as the Gales. I have found that Salt Lake City Mormons are very competitive. You can see a good deal of plastic surgery, especially breast implants. I guess after numerous children, their breasts need to be "re-perk-ified." Krista was real, inside and out, and I was excited to spend time with her. On *erev*—the evening of Rosh Hashanah—I was in a very different kind of Jerusalem.

"Do you mind if I cook for you while I am here?" I asked.

"Mind?" she replied. "We would love that!"

Off to the market we went. I planned to make them brisket, blintzes, matzo ball soup, Mom's Bolognese, and of course, lots of challah.

"I'd like to celebrate the Jewish New Year with you," I told them.

As long as there was food involved, they were on board. I met Krista's mom Pat Miller, who had moved from Phoenix to live with Krista. Pat's husband had died three years before, and she wanted to be closer to family. While there, I found out that not only was her family close, but most of them lived right in the neighborhood, and some on the same block as Krista. It was like *My Big Fat Greek Wedding,* the Mormon edition.

I cooked up a storm. There were pots all over the stove. While the brisket and chicken soup were simmering, I made matzo balls, blintzes, and two flavors of challah: Red Head and Almond Joy Unicorn. When the bread came out of the oven, they devoured it.

"This is incredible!" they exclaimed.

Even Layne loved it. When the food was done cooking, we sat down to dinner.

"I need candles," I said.

There were no Shabbat candles to be found, but Pat located some votives. That would have to do. I knew there wouldn't be wine, but Kurt pulled out some "Mormon champagne" from the fridge. You know that stuff they sell for the kids? Sparkling apple cider! Perfect.

I served the matzo ball soup. I cut up some apples and placed them next to a jar of honey.

"First a few prayers," I told them:

Baruch atah Adonai, Elohenu melech ha'olam, asher kid'shanu b'mitzvotav v'tzivanu l'handlik ner shel Shabbat.

Blessed are You, Lord our G-d, Ruler of the universe, Who has sanctified us with His commandments and commanded us to light the Shabbat candles.

I knew it was Saturday, and this prayer is typically done on Friday night. But Saturday WAS Shabbat, so this should be okay.

The apples!

Baruch atah Adonai, Eloheinu melech ha'olam, borei p'ri ha'eitz.

Blessed are You, Lord our G-d, Ruler of the Universe, Creator of the fruit of the tree. Amen.

Then the champagne.

Baruch atah Adonai, Eloheinu melech ha'olam, borei p'ri hagafen.

We praise G-d, Spirit of Everything, who creates the fruit of the vine. Amen.

The challah:

As my kids had done at Ramat Shalom preschool, I began to sing:

Hamotzi lechem min ha'aretz. We give thanks to G-d for bread. Our voices rise in song together, as our joyful prayer is said. *Baruch atah Adonai, Eloheinu melech ha'olam, hamotzi lechem min ha'aretz. Amen.*

As I was saying these prayers, I thought about the many times in my adult life that reciting prayers—in English or Hebrew—have brought me comfort. I am not religious. Before sending my kids to Jewish pre-k, I didn't know much about my religion, let alone anyone else's. I was a Hebrew school dropout, much to the dismay of my parents. This reminds me of the time Michael and I took a trip to Israel. I was thirty. I was so excited to go that I booked a ten-day tour to make sure we would see all the sights. I found it a little strange that no one on our tour was Jewish. We had two nuns and a priest in our group. We journeyed to Bethlehem, the Church of the Holy Sepulchre, the Church of the Multiplication, the Sea of Galilee. Where were the MOT (members of the tribe)? Maybe I should have studied torah? WHAT WAS WRONG WITH ME?

I asked the tour guide, a young woman named Michal, "When do we get to the Jewish stuff?"

"Jewish stuff? You do know you booked a Christian tour, don't you?" she replied.

WHAT? There are special tours for each religious group? Shari! You work in the travel industry. How did you not know this? Never tell that story to anyone—unless of course you decide to write a memoir where you expose your naivete. Then it will be okay. No judgment please.

I have come to find that the simple act of thanking G-d makes a difference and keeps me grounded. I never dreamed that teaching my Mormon friends some Hebrew prayers would bring me so much joy and inner peace.

Let's eat.

I have found that my Mormon friends LOVE food. Because they have large families, their menus are typically not gourmet. There are a lot of casseroles, macaroni and cheese, stews, chili, Crock-Pot concoctions, pasta, and even something called "bread and with it."

Eldon told me that when he was a kid and the family of eight children was almost out of food for the week, his mom would tell them that dinner was "bread and with it." It was white bread with a side of milk in a bowl and whatever seasoning and leftovers you could find. Yeah, even Eldon said he hated it!

With every bite, Krista, Kurt, and Pat were smiling, salivating, and praising my cooking. They had never seen or eaten a matzo ball. They were in heaven. My brisket is a somewhat strange recipe. The ingredients are a little weird, but the taste is out of this world!

shari's sweet and savory brisket

1 flat brisket, the larger the better because it shrivels up when cooked.

2 cans of whole cranberry sauce

2 15-oz cans of diced tomatoes

6–8 carrots, peeled

celery, washed with the ends cut off

1 liter of ginger ale. Do NOT use diet ginger ale. It has a horrible aftertaste.

head of garlic, diced

1 large Vidalia onion

1 box of chicken or beef broth

olive oil

salt and pepper

g-d bless kurt

Get a large, heavy stockpot—one that you can put in the oven. Le Creuset works great!

Cut the onion into slices.

Peel and chop the garlic or use a few tablespoons from a jar of chopped garlic in oil.

Put the pot on the stove on medium heat. Add in a little bit of oil, the garlic, and the onions. Cook until the onions are a little soft. Move them over to one side of the pot. Remove them if it is easier and add back in later with the other ingredients.

Salt and pepper the brisket and place it into the empty side of the pot. Sear on both sides until brown.

Add in the remaining ingredients. You may not need all the liquid, but you want to add in enough so that the entire brisket is covered. The key to great brisket is for it to be immersed in liquid while it is cooking. Bring it to a simmer and then cover. Turn the burner to low and let it cook on the stove for three and a half hours.

The bigger the brisket, the longer it needs. If you prefer to cook it in the oven, put it in at 350 degrees. Same cooking time. It will cook more quickly in a convection oven.

Once the brisket is done, remove it from the liquid and put it on a platter. Trim the fat. Cover with tinfoil and place it in the refrigerator for a few hours to cool. When you take it out of the fridge, place it on a cutting board and slice it against the grain. If you slice it with the grain, you get what the Cubans call *ropa vieja*—old clothes—or what my mother calls *kvatch*. I think that is Yiddish for total disaster, as the brisket will shred into a gazillion pieces. That will not look good on your holiday table.

Once the liquid cools, skim off the fat. There will be lots of fat! Then take the remaining contents and put in batches into a blender or Vitamix. Puree the liquid into a yummy gravy. Put the gravy into a large container and add in the sliced brisket. Refrigerate. Reheat when ready to serve. Delicious!

As Pat went up the stairs to bed that night, she said, "That was the most incredible day I have had in a very long time. I am so happy you came to visit us."

My cup had runneth over until I picked up my iPhone and saw that Supreme Court Justice Ruth Bader Ginsberg had passed from complications of pancreatic cancer. We were now "Ruth-less." I had prayed for Ruth every day.

Please make it 'til the end of January, dear lady. You have done so much for our country. You are a heroine. If only YOU had been president. You were born too soon. I need you to hang in there for the final furlough.

With each report throughout the past year that she had been hospitalized for infections, broken ribs, and other maladies, I knew her days were numbered. I hoped there were more numbers in her days. I feared for our country before, but not as I had done that day.

Yitgadal v'yitkadash sh'meih raba b'alma di v'ra chiruteih, v'yamlich malchuteih b'chaiyeichon uv'yomeichon uv'chayei d'chol beit Yisrael, ba'agala uviz'man kariv. V'imru:

Amen.

Glorified and sanctified be G-d's great name throughout the world, which He has created according to His will. May He establish His kingdom in your lifetime and during your days, and within the life of the entire House of Israel, speedily, and soon: and say Amen.

Without Ruth, what would our country be like for the next generation of women? Who could replace her? No one. Ruth, may your memory and your work be a blessing for all who knew and loved you. We are all mourning. We all felt as if we knew you, and we most certainly loved you. Rest in power.

Shari's Sweet and Savory Brisket became RBG (Ruth Bader Ginsburg) Brisket—tough yet tender, salty AND sweet, a powerful taste you will never forget!

After dinner I fell into bed. Between the drive from Jackson, the shopping, and the cooking, I was exhausted.

Sunday, September 20, was a rainy day in Salt Lake City. I thought it never rained there, so this was a treat and an opportunity to have some downtime.

Maybe I should start that book?

I took out my computer and started to type. I wrote for hours. I could not stop. All the memories from the Pavilion came flooding back. I had tried to put the past behind me, but I could not do that until it was all chronicled. In between chapters, I cooked a huge pot of my mother's secret Bolognese.

rosie's secret bolognese sauce

4 lbs of lean ground beef

1 lb of sweet Italian sausage, removed from the casings

3 28-ounce cans of tomato sauce

4 bay leaves

dried oregano and other Italian spices

salt and pepper

1 large mozzarella cheese or a bag of shredded mozzarella cheese

olive oil

minced garlic

In a large, heavy stockpot, sauté the garlic in some oil. Use as much garlic as you want.

Add in the ground beef and sausage. Keep chopping the meat until it is in little pieces and browned. There will be about a cup of fat that you have to remove with a turkey baster once the meat is cooked.

Once the meat is somewhat dry, add in everything BUT the cheese.

Cover and cook for ninety minutes on very low heat.

Stir occasionally.

Then comes the magic. Slowly stir in the shredded cheese. If you use a whole mozzarella, you will need to cut it up into small pieces first. Keep stirring until all the cheese has melted into the sauce.

WARNING: your spoon and pot will be a little challenging to clean at the end because there will be some cheese adhered to them. Once you taste this sauce, you will not mind putting a little extra elbow grease into the cleanup.

Spoon over al dente pasta and enjoy. You can add a little shaved parmesan over the top.

This sauce is so good I have been known to just serve myself a bowl and eat it chili style. It doesn't even need pasta! Thanks, Mom!

After I was done cooking, Krista asked if I wanted to join her, Kurt, and Layne on a drive to some of the beautiful sights in the area. I was game for anything. We drove up the mountain to a peaceful meadow with wildflowers and a gorgeous view of the landscape below.

Krista said, "Let's frolic in the grass."

Frolic? I do not frolic.

I had had back surgery on September 12, 2012, after blowing my L5 S1 disc while trying to rescue Michael from a falling garage door. My frolicking days were over. I was happy I could walk without a limp. Krista grabbed me and made me go out into the vast meadow and sing the title song from *The Sound of Music.* I sang at the top of my lungs, as if no one were listening. It felt amazing. It felt freeing. It felt perfect!

Krista put Layne on my shoulders, and we reveled in the tranquility of the moment, until there was crying—Layne, not me. I handed the baby to Kurt, who carried him back to the car. It was time to return to Lehi.

I posted lots of photos of the four of us, with me sporting my favorite denim blue sweatshirt with the words NOT TODAY, SATAN emblazoned across the chest. I had purchased it at a small shop in Minneapolis with Doreen. I usually get dozens of comments on my posts, but none as many as I received that day. I see that Satan plays a big role in the church. Friends of Krista were asking where to buy this item. Friends of friends wanted one! I could have set up a concession in the middle of Salt Lake with this shirt in every size and been sold out in hours. Next visit!

Good thing I had made an enormous pot of sauce, because today the Jacksons were celebrating seventeen-year-old Simone's birthday. Simone is one of Kurt's three kids from his first marriage. A few family members were coming to join us for dinner and birthday cake.

Birthday cake? I love birthday cake.

"What kind of cake?" I asked Krista.

"Ice-cream cake," she said.

I never thought that ice-cream cake was an actual cake. A birthday cake needs flour, frosting, and sprinkles. I had never met Simone, but I was going to bake her a cake from scratch. Back to the market. Flour, food coloring, buttermilk, and many containers of sprinkles. I would make her one of those rainbow cakes where each layer is a different color. I would hollow out the center and fill it with colorful nonpareils and top it with unicorn sprinkles. What a surprise she would get when she cut into it!

"Could we invite Andrew?" I asked.

Andrew had worked with Krista at Morinda. I loved Andrew and would be thrilled to see him again. We called, and he agreed to come.

After my shopping adventure, I started to bake the cake. I found the recipe online. I figured I was up for the challenge.

the best vanilla cake i have ever had

CAKE:

3 and ⅔ cups cake flour (level with a knife)

1 tsp salt

1 tsp baking powder

¾ tsp baking soda

1 and ½ cups unsalted butter, softened to room temperature

2 cups granulated sugar

3 large eggs + 2 additional egg whites, at room temperature

1 tbs pure vanilla extract

1 and ½ cups buttermilk, at room temperature

While making the batter for the cake, I separated it into three bowls. I added green food coloring to one, blue to another, and blue and red to the third. My cake would be green, red, and purple. Everything I need to know I learned in kindergarten!

---

the vanilla buttercream frosting

1 and ½ cups unsalted butter, softened to room temperature.

6 cups confectioners' sugar

⅓ cup whole milk or heavy cream

1 and ½ tsp pure vanilla extract

⅛ tsp salt

Pink coloring is done by adding in red food dye to the frosting, just enough to make it pink, and not too much so that it turns bright red.

INSTRUCTIONS:

Preheat oven to 350 degrees. Grease three nine-inch cake pans, line with parchment paper, then grease the parchment paper. Parchment paper helps the cakes seamlessly release from the pans.

MAKE THE CAKE:

Whisk the cake flour, salt, baking powder, and baking soda together. Set aside.

Using a handheld or stand mixer fitted with a paddle or whisk attachment, beat the butter and sugar together on high speed until smooth and creamy, about three minutes. Scrape down the sides and up the bottom of the bowl with a rubber spatula as needed.

Beat in the three eggs, two egg whites, and vanilla extract on high speed until combined, about two minutes. The mixture will look curdled because of the egg liquid and solid butter combining. Scrape down the sides and up the bottom of the bowl as needed. With the mixer on low speed, add the dry ingredients just until combined.

With the mixer still running on low, pour in the buttermilk, and mix just until combined. You may need to whisk it all by hand to make sure there are no lumps at the bottom of the bowl. The batter will be slightly thick.

Pour batter evenly into cake pans. Bake for around twenty-three to twenty-six minutes or until the cakes are baked through. To test for doneness, insert a toothpick into the center of the cake. If it comes out clean, it's done. Allow cakes to cool completely in the pans set on a wire rack. The cakes must be completely cool before frosting and assembling.

MAKE THE FROSTING:

In a large bowl, using a handheld mixer or stand mixer fitted with a whisk or paddle attachment, beat the butter on medium speed until creamy, about two minutes. Add confectioners' sugar, milk, vanilla extract, and salt with the mixer running on low.

Increase to high speed and beat for two minutes. Add more confectioners' sugar if frosting is too thin, more milk if frosting is too thick, or an extra pinch of salt if frosting is too sweet.

ASSEMBLE AND DECORATE:

I stacked the three layers of the cake—with the frosting in between—and covered the sides with the balance of the rosy-colored buttercream. Once the layers were stacked and frosted, I took a knife and carved a circular trench through the middle. As I dug cake out of the inside, I ate it! It was delicious! I poured nonpareils into the abyss and frosted over it. Once the entire cake was covered in frosting, I put it in the sink and poured unicorn sprinkles—a container of every imaginable type of sprinkle and sparkling sugar—over the top and sides of the cake.

Refrigerate the cake for at least 1 hour before slicing. This helps the cake hold its shape when cutting.

It was a masterpiece, and I couldn't wait to see Simone's face when she cut into it. Actually, I couldn't wait to see Simone's face. Remember, I had never met her!

Guests started to arrive. First, Mike and Rebecca. Mike is Krista's brother. He was moving from Phoenix to Salt Lake City to be closer to family. With them would come seven of their fourteen children. Yes, you read that right. Rebecca is forty-six and has given birth to TEN of the fourteen. The remaining four are from Mike's first marriage. Rebecca and Mike are grandparents to several kids as well!

Simone arrived with her brother and sister. Then Kendra and Kevin, Mike and Rebecca's daughter and son-in-law. Then Bobby Jo and Kerm (Kurt's parents). The parade of people did not stop. We were in the middle of a pandemic, and there were at least forty house guests. Kasey (Kurt's brother) and his fiancée Taylor, Kade (Kurt's cousin), Brooke and Derek, Brinley, Zacc, and more.

I started to panic. I remembered that, like the Duggars, (who incidentally are not part of the church), Mormon families have a habit of picking one letter and giving each kid a name that begins with that letter. Kurt, Kasey, Kade. You get the idea. They also change the spelling of traditional names as Rebecca and Mike had done with their daughter Ashlie, and make up others as with their son, Kylen. Kurt's other siblings are Kelsi and Kamie. There are many Mormon kids named Brindsey, Brindslie, Bryleigh, Brynlee, and Brailee. No one can find a mug with their name on it at Disney World.

And I thought Shari was impossible!

If I ever hear a Mormon poke fun at a Black family, I will go postal. Mormon surnames tend to be very traditional and American-sounding: Miller, Tanner, Gale, Young, which is a good thing since some have a tradition of giving their children their mother's maiden name as a middle name, hence

Layne Miller Jackson. Krista's maiden name is Miller. It is a lot to keep straight.

I sat and watched the interaction of the multitude of guests. They all knew each other. Heck. They were all related! There were no gifts other than the few that Pat gave Simone. If you are not following, Pat is Simone's grandmother by marriage—Kurt to Krista. I suppose it would be impossible to give each relative a birthday present when your immediate family is dozens of people. Simone opened the small package. Inside were two items, both made by the same company, Aloha.

There was a makeup bag, and a fanny pack made of a washable parachute material. I thought these were great! Pat told me she buys several at a time online so that she always has gifts handy. With so many relatives, this is the way to go!

Finally, Andrew arrived. He was the only guest I knew. He had been part of the church but left years ago.

"The whole *mishpucha* is here!" he shouted.

"Andrew! How do you know that word?" I asked.

"Hey, I watched *The Nanny*!" he replied proudly.

The kitchen was set up like a buffet. I watched everyone enjoy Mom's Bolognese sauce. People took seconds. They scarfed down the challah and the two loaves of Italian bread I had found the time to make hours earlier. Krista bought me Everything But the Bagel spice, and I poured it all over the loaves. I heard the guests asking, "Who made this pasta sauce?" I was beaming with pride. Everyone wanted to meet the outsider. I was a celebrity chef! The Jewish Julia Childs, but with a sense of humor and a sassy New York accent.

After dinner, we presented Simone with the cake. I had put it in the refrigerator because the frosting was made with butter and cream. It had shifted a bit and had become a bit of a leaning tower but was better than any cake I had ever made.

We put seventeen candles on the cake. We sang happy birthday. Simone was beaming and blew out the candles. I think blowing out the candles on a cake is now outlawed due to COVID. At this point I had been in a house with forty strangers. I could not interview them on their whereabouts. I WAS eating that cake! Perhaps my O+ blood has kept me immune from this disease anyway. Simone cut into the cake. The sprinkles poured out.

The guests were in awe. It was magic. I bet Simone will never forget this birthday.

As Krista and Pat were cleaning up, Kurt and some of the guys were in the living room, talking. I could overhear the conversation, especially the words AR15, which caught my attention.

"Did someone just say AR15?" I asked.

"Yes," replied Kurt. "Do you want to see one?"

"You HAVE an AR15?" I exclaimed.

"I have three guns. That is just one of them. They are upstairs in cases underneath the bed," he added.

I thought for sure he was pulling my leg. "Yeah, sure. I want to see the weapon that ruined the lives of seventeen innocent people and their families in Parkland near my home," I said.

Up the stairs we went into one of the guest bedrooms. I still thought Kurt was kidding. He crouched down, put his hands underneath the bed, and produced three gun cases. Oh my G-d. He really had guns!

"Everyone around here has guns," he explained.

I knew lots of people in red states were passionate about the Second Amendment, but I had never seen or held a gun except for those squirt guns you get at a carnival where you aim for the little target to blow up and break a balloon and get a prize. I was never very good at it, which is why my childhood bedroom was never full of poor-quality stuffed animals.

Kurt opened the cases and handed me one of the guns.

"Is this the AR15?" I asked hesitantly.

"No, this is a smaller one, and don't worry, it's not loaded," he said.

Gee! That's a plus! I held the gun in my hands. He showed me how to aim. I felt oddly empowered with this unloaded weapon. The second gun was a hunting rifle. "Where is the AR15? I want to see it," I asked.

Kurt removed a larger gun from a case. It was scary looking. This was it. The gun that had ripped loved ones from their families. Pulse Night Club, Mandalay Bay in Vegas, Parkland, and countless others. This was a weapon of mass destruction. This was the weapon Americans could just purchase without being soldiers in a deadly war. Kurt handed me the AR15. It weighed about seven pounds but felt like twenty.

"May I ask why you have these guns, Kurt?" I wondered.

"Everyone around here has guns," he replied.

I went back in my mind to a phrase I have used many times in business.

g-d bless kurt

You may have the right to do something, but is it the right thing to do?

As I continued to hold the AR15, I turned around and saw one-year-old Layne walking toward the bedroom, and I imagined, could this innocent, blue-eyed boy or a friend of his find these guns one day and become school shooters? The thought was frightening. Was having guns in the house the right thing to do?

I handed the gun to Kurt and said, "Please put these away. I never want to see one again."

I left the bedroom, grabbed Layne, and went downstairs. I didn't shoot a gun, but I felt guilty of committing a crime. The only firearm in the Jackson house that I had enjoyed using was a yellow plastic rifle that killed bugs with air-charged salt. I must get one for Hanukkah!

Before going to bed, Pat found me sitting on the couch in the living room.

"I have something for you," she said. "I want to give you a gift."

Give ME a gift? I thought. *Wow. Okay.*

Pat opened a bag, and inside were several of the same fanny packs and makeup bags that she had given Simone.

"Please, pick one of each," Pat said.

I chose two bags with nautical patterns on them. I was honored and thrilled with my gifts. I hadn't brought a makeup bag with me on the trip, mostly because I didn't bring any makeup. I had so many little items: a tweezer, perfume, deodorant, Q-tips, and toothpaste, which all fit perfectly into the larger of the two bags. The second was the lightest fanny pack ever produced. The waterproof parachute material was perfect.

The following morning, I taught a challah baking class on Facebook Live. While I do these sessions, I talk about my journey and where I am headed next. While on this session, I got a text from Lili Gaudreau from San Francisco. She, her husband Stephane, and I had worked together at Club Med dozens of years before.

The text read, "You are going to Zion Wednesday? The kids, Stephane, and I will be there too! Let's meet!"

Awesome! I would not be alone in southern Utah. I decided this was the time to try glamping. I had heard about it and wanted to experience it. I booked a tent, with a king-sized bed, at Zions View Camping in Hildale for two nights. I thought it would be close to the park. At the same time, I booked an Airbnb near Bryce Canyon for one night immediately following the glamp! I also decided to fly to Los Angeles on September 26. It did not seem right to be in

Utah for Yom Kippur. I would meet my friend Wendy Hallin for dinner, then drive down to Costa Mesa to see friends in Orange County.

Wendy is the niece of both Garry and Penny Marshall of *Happy Days* and *Laverne and Shirley* fame. We had met back in 2001 in Positano, Italy, when I was dining with Michael at a restaurant called Bucca di Bacco. Wendy was traveling with her friend Kathy. They were enjoying a fruit-plate dessert with large pieces of cantaloupe. Mike looked over at them and said, "Nice melons," and a new friendship was born.

Before I headed to Zion, I wanted to visit my friend Lynn Lee, her husband Mike, and their black lab, Scallywag. They have a town house in the middle of Deer Valley, adjacent to Park City. I drove an hour up the mountain. I could feel my face and lips getting chapped. I kept drinking water, but it did not help. My skin was flaking off. What I needed was an entire-body sugar scrub!

Mike and Lynn met me at a pub downtown. The old-fashioned with Luxardo cherries was magnificent. I wanted to have a second, but I would have collapsed at the table. Lynn and I shared some wild salmon, which was delicious. I remembered why I much prefer Pacific salmon over the Atlantic farmed variety. The taste is so different and far less fatty. It was served to us hot and crispy, accompanied by pan-fried gnocchi, corn, and asparagus. Sensational. We shared some sliced beef tacos too. As much as I wanted to see the dessert menu, I was stuffed.

We drove to the town house and were greeted by a large personalized welcome sign and two-year-old Scallywag, who quickly realized that I love dogs. I unknowingly sat in his spot on the couch, and he positioned himself on top of me. Scallywag is eighty pounds of pure puppy love. He has no personal boundaries. He will share your food. He will put his paw on your leg when you are not paying attention to him as if to say, "Hey, you are in my house. Let's play NOW!" I really liked him. The feeling was mutual.

"Want to learn how to make challah?" I asked Lynn.

"Right now? At 9:00 p.m.?" she replied.

"No time like the present," I said. I had brought the bread flour and yeast with me from Salt Lake City. We baked a traditional challah.

Lynn and Mike tasted it. "WOW! This is delicious," they exclaimed.

"I will make you a custom challah tomorrow. What would you like in your bread?" I asked.

"Can you make it with cranberries?" Lynn requested.

"Sure!" I said. "I will pick up some cranberries and other surprises tomorrow. Can I cook for you tomorrow night?" I asked Lynn.

"Absolutely. We don't cook a lot," she said.

After a lovely night's sleep in the most delicious bed, I woke up on Tuesday morning and headed to the market. That night, I would make rack of lamb, oven-roasted truffle broccoli, and acorn squash with truffle salt, butter, and honey. We'd have a green salad with Stonewall Kitchen Bacon Vinaigrette. For dessert I would make them Grammy Esther's cheese blintzes with sour cream and sugar. I had made the blintzes in advance so that I had to only pan fry them later. Everything else would be prepared a la minute.

Before I did anything else, I wanted to make that cranberry challah for Lynn. Cranberries by themselves would not make for a very exciting bread. What if I made a tie-dyed cranberry, chocolate, coconut bread? I bet she would love that. I threw together the ingredients, let the dough rise, braided it, and put it in the oven. When it came out, Lynn's eyes were wide with delight.

"Do you know what I call this bread, Lynn?" I asked her.

"Scallywag?" she responded.

Exactly!

Lynn and I decided it would be nice to have a mani/pedi in the late afternoon. We went to her favorite salon in town. The $45 pedicure was heaven. It included a fifteen-minute hand and stone massage, a clay leg mask, and a paraffin wax treatment. It was well worth the money. I was so relaxed that I didn't know how I was going to stand to prepare dinner.

We stopped at a place called Cole Sports, where I bought a pair of hiking boots, a biking helmet, and a CamelBak. I needed the new helmet to go with the new Rollerblades that would be waiting for me in Florida. The boots and the water pouch would be great in Zion and Bryce.

When I got home, I took the $57 rack of lamb out of the refrigerator. When I unwrapped the wax paper, I was surprised to find that the butcher had cut the rack into chops. Oh no! Without a barbecue, I had no idea how to cook lamb chops. I know only how to bake the entire rack as one piece. I set the oven to 350 degrees and decided to cook the ribs on a baking pan. I had no idea how much grease this was going to produce. It was fortunate that the baking pan had sides to hold in the fatty liquid, or I would have ruined Lynn's new kitchen and probably have caused the town house to burn down.

I put the cut broccoli into a large bowl, adding olive oil and some truffle salt. I put it on a baking sheet and placed it into the oven. I pierced the acorn squash several times and placed it on a microwave-safe plate. I nuked it for ten minutes, removed it, halved it, and took out the seeds. Then I placed the two halves of squash, skin-side down, on a baking sheet. I put a tablespoon of butter inside each, added a tablespoon of honey, and a sprinkle of truffle salt. I added this to the oven.

The vegetables were cooking nicely, but the lamb chops were swimming in lamb grease. UGH. I took them out, drained the fat, turned the chops over, and set them back in the oven. After ten minutes on each side, I assumed they were done. They did not look like anything I would feature in a cookbook, but I bet they would taste fine.

We sat down for dinner. Everything was delicious. The lamb did not look restaurant-worthy, but it tasted exquisite. Once my father told me that it is hard to ruin a great piece of meat, unless you cook it well done. These chops were medium, pink, and perfect!

Before Lynn and Mike could finish their entrees, I got to work in the kitchen preparing dessert. I cut up strawberries, raspberries, and blackberries. I slathered the plate with some huckleberry jam that I had brought them as part of a thank-you gift. I placed two hot and crispy pan-fried blintzes on each plate. Then I added a dollop of full-fat sour cream, and topped it with granulated sugar. I finished by decorating the plate with the sliced berries.

When I put the plate in front of Mike, he said, "This looks wonderful, but I don't know if I can eat another bite."

Seconds later, the plate was clean. Lynn and Mike were now in a food coma. I froze the remaining blintzes. Soon they could impress their friends! I know that someday I will return and make another batch!

chapter eleven

a jew goes to zion

I got up early to drive to Springdale. I wanted to connect with the Gaudreau family by lunch. I was on the open road, singing Broadway show tunes at the top of my lungs. No one was in the car to tell me to lower my voice or change the station.

My favorite performer by far has always been Carole King. Smart, successful, Jewish, bold, talented, and from what I could tell by watching her sing – insightful, kind, and authentic.

Wouldn't she be the ultimate Passover guest? Perhaps one day she will accept my invite.

As a kid, I knew the lyrics to every single one of her songs. I still do. As I drove, I could hear the words to one of my favorites whirling around my brain. I thought about my life and it's "rich and royal hue." I had certainly come a long way since my modest, lower middle-class upbringing. Since then, I have created my own unique tapestry, woven with people, places, and experiences. I've always had an "everlasting vision of the ever-changing view." My father told me that the only sure thing in life is change. Well, he also mentioned death and taxes, but I prefer to embrace change, pay the taxes, and not contemplate death.

I remember when I was a kid and wore out my Carole King eight tracks.

Remember eight tracks?

I had some tough times in my childhood, and her music helped me escape. We had everything we needed financially to survive, but emotionally I was often empty. Because of that I became needy. I did not know how to make friends. I was socially awkward and attached myself to anyone who would let me. I needed to be the center of attention, and I know I wasn't the best listener.

Through the years I have learned that making a friend means being a friend. I do my best to listen attentively, be empathetic, and focus on giving rather than receiving. I share almost everything I have as I have found little happiness in enjoying things alone. Music was my escape during my childhood, and now it was providing me with peace, comfort, and company. Singing Carole King songs has always made me feel good:

> Sometimes I wonder if I'm ever gonna make it home again.
> It's so far and out of sight.
>
> I really need someone to talk to
> And nobody else knows how to comfort me tonight.
>
> Snow is cold. Rain is wet.
> Chills my soul right to the marrow.
> I won't be happy 'til I see you alone again.
> 'Til I'm home again and feeling right.

But did I want to go home? I WAS feeling right. Did I need to see the people I had left behind? I was happy away. Could I go back and stay joyful? Was it the place that had made me sad? Was it the people? Was it the business? What was the key to going back home and bringing this newly improved self with me?

I still had a few more weeks and more people to visit. I was not going to worry about it just yet, but I will admit, I was anxious. I kept singing and driving my black Nissan Sentra. Not the most luxurious car, but I was renting it and not buying it, so it was just fine. I was in my own world, whirling down the freeway on the way to Zion. Why would they call a place in Utah, Zion? Doesn't Zion mean Israel? I asked Siri to find me the information:

The park was originally a season camping ground for the Paiute Indians but was settled by Mormons in the 1850s, who farmed the area and named it

Zion, which means "place of refuge." A good name if you have had occasion to visit because it is a natural fortress, and the Mormons, who had been driven west by mobs and general persecution, saw themselves as refugees. In fact, Mormons still informally refer to Utah as "Zion," the same way Jews view Israel as Zion.

I can't wait to get to Zion! Perhaps I, too, am a refugee.

I continued to sail down the freeway with visions of greatness dancing in my head when I randomly checked the rear-view mirror. There was a cop behind me in a car with flashing lights. I needed to move over so that he could get to his emergency, wherever it was. I moved to the right lane, and he followed me. Uh-oh. I guessed I had been going over the speed limit. I pulled over to the shoulder. Shit! I had just seen *The Hate U Give*. Khalil gets killed for getting out of the car and reaching for his cell phone.

Shari, put your hands at ten and two. Do not move. You are not a Black man, but what if this guy doesn't like New Yorkers?

I wasn't taking any chances. Once the car was parked, I lowered the window, and I put my hands into position. A fat, short, bald, white "doughnut cop" walked over to my car. I did not move.

"Is there any reason why you would be driving this out of control?" asked Officer Barnett.

I smiled. "Not really," I replied.

Gee, I thought I had been perfectly in control.

"I clocked you at one hundred and six miles per hour," he told me.

Does a Nissan Sentra even GO one hundred and six miles per hour?

I was impressed with myself and the car. "I suppose I was in my own world," I told him.

"I have been tracking you for five minutes, and you didn't pull over," Barnett lectured.

Really? It took your V8 a whole FIVE minutes to catch my little econocar?

"And in THIS WORLD, the speed limit is eighty. I am going to have to issue you a citation," he said. "License and registration."

I wanted to be sarcastic and ask him if he was selling tickets to the state policeman's ball, but I figured this guy did not have a sense of humor, and I did not want to be in further trouble.

Oh . . . and a citation? Really? In this world don't they still call that a speeding ticket?

He was a vanilla-white, bald doughnut cop. He returned to his Dodge Durango for a bit, came back, and handed me the citation. Three hundred and eighty dollars.

Ouch! Then he read the instructions to me so that I would know how to pay for said citation.

What? Don't people in Utah read? I can read it myself, thank you very much.

I smiled at him and thanked him for the ticket. He gave me more fodder to write about. Getting upset would not change a thing.

He drove away.

I sat there for a moment.

What if I were a Black man? It probably would have been worse and maybe more expensive. That sucks. Will it ever change?

I got back on the road, headed for Zion. I would call a local attorney and see if I could get out of the ticket. I had done that in Florida once. I should be able to do it in Utah, right? So, I called a lawyer and was told that they take tickets very seriously in Beaver. He advised me to call the prosecutor's office and said that I'd probably be calling him back to happily pay him $500 to get the fine reduced by $100.

Well, that made no sense. It was a $380 ticket. He would reduce it to $280, and I would have to pay him $500 for the privilege? Not happening.

"Hello? My name is Shari Wallack, and I was going one hundred and six in an eighty. Can you help me?"

The voice on the other end sounded like a cross between Barney Fife from *The Andy Griffith Show* and Eeyore. Same tone, accent, and s-l-o-w pace.

"This is Leo. Let me see what I can do," he said.

"Do you need the citation number?" I asked.

"No, I found you," he replied.

Wow, this must be one heck of a small town!

"Well, you WERE doing one hundred and six in an eighty, and that is not acceptable. I don't think I can do much. My boss is going to make you pay, and I can't get you out of the points on your license. You were going pretty fast," he said.

"Yes, I know. I don't usually speed. I was just so amazed by the fabulous scenery in Utah. It's my first time here! Is there anything you can do?" I asked sweetly.

"Well, maybe I can reduce the speed by ten miles and put down that you were only going sixteen miles over. Yeah, I think I can do that. How do you feel about the fine? Three hundred and eighty dollars is a lot of money," he said.

"Yes, it is. Is there anything you can do?" I pleaded.

"Well, my boss won't let me reduce it by much, but how do you feel about $210? Does that sound okay?" he asked.

Is this really happening? How do I feel about it? Well, I feel shitty! I don't want to pay anything, but I can pay the $210 and put this behind me.

"That is awesome, Leo," I exclaimed. "Thank you so much. So, when do I pay the $210?" I asked.

"Well, give me a few minutes, and I will go into the system and change the amount. Once you go on the website and see that it was reduced, you can pay it," he said.

It was almost worth the fine and the few points I would get on my license for this adventure. No more speeding for me in Beaver!

I arrived at Springdale and met Lili and Stephane at the pool of their hotel. We discussed the afternoon and evening plans. They went on a hike in the park. I decided to get a massage at a nearby spa. It was heavenly, even masked.

I returned to the hotel to join the family for dinner. We ate at the Bit and Spur across the street. I highly recommend the salmon tacos! I looked at my watch. It was 9:30 p.m., and I had to get to my tent in the woods. I thought it was just a few miles away. But when I put the address into Google Maps, it was fifty minutes down the road, in the dark. I had to leave immediately, before my glass slipper fell off!

Into the wilderness I drove. The GPS would take me only to an intersection in Hildale. I would have to follow texted directions and a hand-written map from there to my tent at Zions View Camping. I admit, I was a little nervous. I was going to spend two nights by myself in a tent in the mountains. No electricity, running water, or Wi-Fi. At least there would be a king-sized bed in my tent, and they told me the bathroom was nearby. I could put my merit badges to good use! An adventure.

After getting lost on the dirt road, I finally found the campsite and my tent. Each tent had a name. Mine was Lone Rock. I was Lone Shari. Awesome! I drove the car right up to the tent, using the car's headlights to guide me to the entrance. It looked so serene. I walked to this yurt and opened the zippers. The inside was like something out of a Harrison Ford movie. I felt as if I were filming *Raiders of the Lost Ark*. There was a pole holding up the middle of the tent. There was ample room with a king-sized bed, five pillows, and an extra blanket. To the left were two chairs, a night table, and two towels. Oh good, tomorrow I could take a shower before heading out.

On another table, I saw two battery-operated lanterns, a triangle-shaped hazard light, and a headlamp. There was a box of tissues, and next to it, a pouch of wet wipes. Wet wipes? I suppose in lieu of hand sanitizer. Outside I found a firepit, some wood, a charcoal grill, a picnic table, a few chairs, and a big blue container of drinking water. There were three additional items: a lighter, lighter fluid, and BBQ tongs.

It was 10:45 p.m. I just wanted to go to bed, but I had to make a campfire. I love the smell of burning wood. I put on my Snoopy pajamas, placed the bone-dry logs into the pit, sprayed them with that fluid that reminds me of cookouts on Fire Island, ignited the soaked wood with a butane lighter, and reveled in my firepit masterpiece. I sat beside it until it the last ember burned out.

Proud of myself, not so much for the fire, but for finding the tent in the dark, I got into bed and passed out. Fortunately, I had used the restroom at the Bit and Spur and would not have to go again until sunrise.

It is probably inappropriate to talk about one's bathroom habits, but you need to know about mine to understand the next part. At 6:30 a.m. I woke up as I do every morning. It was dark. It was cold. I needed to go. I have never been constipated a day in my life. I can eat boxes of matzo at Passover and am still regular. I never understood that joke they tell at seder time about Moses asking the Pharaoh to "Let my people go!" I can always go.

Okay, I would look for the bathroom. I didn't see one anywhere near my tent. In the distance, I saw a blue Porta Potty.

Seriously? Was THAT the bathroom?

I would have to trek down the hill in my Snoopy pajamas to poop in a toilet that stank and didn't flush? Not happening! If a bear can . . . I will be a bear!

I took off my bottoms and, with my trusty headlight attached, I looked for a good spot. I would have to hold onto something or risk falling. There it was! A big rock right next to my tent. I grabbed a few of those wet wipes, walked over, squatted, and held onto the rock. I did it! I was so proud of myself. I didn't fall. I wiped, stood up, and headed back toward the tent. In my post-poop glory, I forgot that I had walked a bit uphill to get to "doody rock." I tripped and fell on my newly wiped behind. Normally, this would not be a big deal, but I was naked from the waist down, and the ground was covered in sandstone.

Sandstone is a powdery red clay, which instantly adheres itself to wet skin, like when you go to a fine-sand beach, swim, and then try to lie down on your towel, only your body overflows. You get the picture. It was dark. I had no idea where the shower was. I should go back to bed for another hour. I reentered the tent. I grabbed some wet wipes and gave myself a poor version of a sponge bath. The more I wiped, the more I began to look like an indigenous person. The wipes were filthy, and so was I. I was never going to get all the sandstone off. I decided to wait for the sun to rise. Then I would find the shower, and this would all be a faint memory.

7:30 a.m. I put on some dirty clothes. It was maybe forty degrees out. I did not care. I had to get that red dust off me. I walked around a bit, holding some shampoo and a towel. There it was. The shower. Thank goodness! I walked over to it and opened the door. SHIT! This was not an actual shower. It was a sun shower. There was a flimsy seat and two black pouches that looked like large IV bags hanging on the wall. Apparently, the sun warms the sacks, and you squirt the solar-heated water all over yourself until you are clean.

I was NOT doing this. The water was likely frigid from sitting out there overnight, and I was not going to stand outside, naked, in slightly warmer than freezing air, hoping that the shampoo was gone before the water. Forget it!

I got in the car and drove to Lili's hotel. I went to Meme's Café for breakfast to eat and wait for the Gaudreaus to awaken. I ordered coffee and a breakfast crepe. The server returned with my breakfast and a mug of coffee. Much to my delight and surprise, the mug said "Good Morning Sunshine" on both sides. I looked around to see if others had the same mug and was not shocked to see that mine was the only one. Everyone else had a plain white cup. It was a sign.

Arnon had been sending me red cardinals since his passing. Now, Michael Hurwitz, my first mentor, who had died two years ago, following a bout with lung cancer, was making an appearance. Whenever I called Michael through the years, he would answer the phone and say, "Hello, Sunshine." He was the only person in my life to ever call me Sunshine. The first time I went to Tahiti, I asked the locals for the translation for sunshine, because I wanted to adopt an accurate Polynesian name. Mahana!

"That's you!" they told me enthusiastically! "Mahana!"

I have been back to Tahiti a few times and always embrace my inner Mahana! With the delivery of my mug, I knew I was still on the right road. I do not normally take things from restaurants, but I had to have this mug. I waited for the waitress to come back. She never did.

I left $20 on the table, wiped out the mug with a thin napkin, and placed it into my bag. Since G-d did not smite me for taking rocks near Yellowstone, He probably would give me a pass for lifting a $5 cup!

At a human hour, I called Lili and asked to use her shower. It never felt so good to have hot water running down my body. I watched the red dirt slide off my skin and into the tub, which looked like a murder scene. Blood-colored water everywhere. I stayed in that shower for fifteen minutes. Thank goodness the Gaudreau family was in town. Otherwise, it could have been a very uncomfortably dirty day.

The family and I walked around the town for a bit before heading to Coral Pink Sand Dunes State Park for an ATV tour. If you google it, you will find that this park is listed as having the coolest sand dunes in the United States. We boarded our vehicles for a one-hour tour. It was exhilarating. I can describe it only as a combination snowmobile and roller-coaster ride. But in the sand!

We were flying over the dunes. There were hills, valleys, and sand as far as the eye could see. It was the first time I was happy I was wearing a face mask in addition to the provided goggles, because the dunes are as dry as a bone, and the sand becomes airborne. When we were done, I was covered in coral dust. Oh GREAT! Here we go again!

I bid my friends goodbye and drove back to the tent in Hildale. I decided it would be best to find a restaurant in town before making another campfire and retiring for the evening. Not knowing the area, I stopped into Paty's Place—yes one "t"—to ask for some recommendations. As I entered the shop, right there in front of me was a rack of handmade dishtowels. The one on display featured a red cardinal. I was going to go wherever Paty told me to!

"Well, there are a few restaurants in town," she said. "Try Edge of the World Brewery."

Well, that sounded exotic. Why not?

"Where is the town?" I asked her.

"Just go down Utah Avenue, then turn this way and that way, and you cannot miss it!" Paty explained.

When someone tells me that I can't miss something, it is a recipe for *Lost*! I bought the dishtowel and got back into the car. I drove around and around and around. Where was this town? There was nothing but dirt and a few houses. No one was in the street. My GPS did not work. I found a high school, a few closed businesses, and a tiny supermarket that was not open.

I got out of the car and looked around. THERE! I saw a window sign that said Edge of the World Brewery. There were a few cars in the parking lot. I went inside. This place was a far cry from *Cheers*. It was a boxy room with concrete floors, empty walls, two large-screen televisions mounted on opposing sides, card tables with chairs, a cash register, and a bar. There was an empty blackboard that did not list any specials. There was no liquor in the bar, considering the Mormon clientele, but they did serve beer and a few ciders.

The Lucite stands sitting on the bar and tables sported a description of the following items: a variety of pizzas in different sizes, chicken wings, a giant pretzel, jalapeño poppers, artichoke dip with chips, and nachos. I was alone, so I sat at the bar. Molly, a native of New Mexico and the only waitress in the joint, asked if I wanted to order something. I requested the dinner menu. Molly pointed to the Lucite stand and said, "That IS the dinner menu."

WHAT? It was bowling alley food. THAT was dinner?

"Would you like a drink?" she asked.

"I like cider," I said.

In honor of Claire Gale, I would try the pineapple cider. How bad could it be? I took a cautious sip. It was pretty good. Molly asked if I wanted to order food.

Okay. "I will have a five-inch Margherita pizza and a basket of wings," I told her.

"What kind?" she asked me. "We have Essie's BBQ, spicy buffalo, and salt/pepper seasoned.

I wanted to know who Essie was, but I was tired and hungry. "I will have seasoned," I told her.

I sat at the bar and looked around. The restaurant was full, with more people waiting outside. They all knew each other. Of course, they did! They were probably related.

This might have been the only open restaurant in Hildale. The population there is twenty-nine hundred. Everyone else was probably dining in that night! I sipped my pineapple cider. I waited for my food. The glass was empty. Fifteen minutes passed. Molly came over to me with a big smile.

"Did you order food?" she asked me.

Uh . . . didn't she take my order?

"Yes, didn't you write it down?" I asked her.

"I don't remember. Let me look through my notes," she said.

She pulled out a little notebook, like the ones kids used to carry in their school bags to keep track of important information back in the seventies and eighties. She flipped through the pages and searched for my order.

"Oh yes, I remember now," she said.

It's not as if I had anywhere to be.

I smiled and told her it was fine. Eventually my food came out. The wings were hot and delicious. The pizza was interesting, better than Ellio's frozen, but not by much. The tomatoes were the tiny cherry variety, sliced in half. The crust was soft, wilted, and laden with far too much sauce and cheese. I ate what I could, left the rest, and headed back to Lone Rock.

Along the way, I picked up a bundle of firewood. I was looking forward to sitting by the campfire and recounting more of my journey on my trusty Dell laptop. I changed into my Snoopies, ignited the wood like a pro, and positioned myself on the metal chair next to the fire pit. There was silence. The stars were bright. It was pitch black. I was alone, but far from lonely. I would have been unhappy to have anyone infringe upon my private time. I did not want to talk. I did not want to entertain anyone. I did not want a soul to interrupt or reroute my journey. The last thing I wanted to do was check my iPhone for news, social media, texts, or emails.

Who IS this person?

I used to get high on the ding produced when I got a new message. Now I was out here in the wilderness, happy that no one could find me. I was with my most interesting travel companion, and she was writing the next *Wild* or perhaps *Untamed.*

When the fire extinguished itself and the temperature outside dipped to fifty, it was time to crawl into my tented king bed for the last time. I brushed my teeth with bottled water, put on a pair of hand-knit slippers I had purchased at Paty's Place, and got under the covers.

Before I fell asleep, I reflected on the raging pandemic. People were sitting by their large-screen TVs intoxicated with political advertisements and COVID numbers. Many were out of work and financially strapped. Families were having a rough time continuing to quarantine. The governor of Florida, Ron DeSantis, had moved our state into phase three, which would surely lead to an increased number of cases and deaths. The travel industry was diligently trying to convince corporations and individuals that the proper protocols were in place to allow everyone to fly and safely stay at hotels. The cruise industry was up in arms because other modes of vacation had returned to service, yet passenger ships were still docked and empty. And what about the elderly, their golden years put on hold? They were living through this time, just hoping to hug their grandchildren again.

So much had been lost in 2020. Halloween would surely be canceled. Thanksgiving, the day of my fifty-seventh birthday, would not look the same. The Macy's Thanksgiving Day Parade, my favorite televised event next to the Tony Awards, might be canceled. And for those who celebrate Christmas, this would be a strange year. Retailers make most of their money between Thanksgiving and Christmas. Would they survive? Not unless they had a huge online presence. No big New Year's Eve parties. When would this end? Would it take a year and a half like the Spanish flu? How many more would die?

Friday, September 25, my internal alarm clock woke me up. Time to visit poop rock for the last time. I was so much more experienced now! Am I crazy, or is it freeing to relieve one's self in the woods? Maybe there is a reason why some say "nature calls" when they "have to go."

This was as close as I could get to nature. I find it funny that the queen of England calls it a "comfort break." If she were with me at "doody point," she would find nothing comfortable about it! First, Queen Elizabeth would never be glamping. Second, if she were, she would have to hold it in until arriving back in the UK.

I packed up my things and drove to Bryce Canyon. I chose to book an afternoon tour as I had done in Jackson Hole. With time to spare, I went to the general store. I bought T-shirts, a mug, a native flute, some gifts, and the only red cardinal bird feeder in the shop. Perfect! I had bags of stuff and asked the cashier where the nearest post office was. She pointed to a kiosk inside the store.

WOW! The post office was just a few feet away. There, I met Sandy, the postal clerk. Sandy was a heavyset lady with white hair and a bad limp. I figured she was in her late sixties. I walked over and introduced myself. I wanted to have a relationship with Sandy so that she would help me pack up the gifts and send them to their respective recipients. I could hardly get her to crack a smile. She seemed annoyed with me. I was making her work. I tried everything I could to engage with her. I thanked her profusely for helping me. I called her a rock star. I told her she was fabulous. Still, she was sliding postage labels underneath the plexiglass with a bit of an attitude.

I wasn't getting anywhere with Sandy. I thanked her anyway and left. I went out to the car. I grabbed a bag of sticks and rocks I had collected on the road during the past few days. I would mail these to Dan, and he could make some fun nature chains for himself. I bought Dan another mug and an awesome T-shirt sporting a neat cartoon of a VW. I walked back to Sandy.

"Have you missed me?" I joked.

"It's only been a few minutes. How could I miss you?" said Sandy with a straight face.

"Do you have a box long enough to ship these items?" I asked her.

"Nope. That will not fit in any of my boxes," she replied stoically.

"Okay, I will remove the longest stick," I suggested.

With that, she produced the perfect box.

I said, "I knew you could find me something, Sandy. You are my hero."

She started to crack a smile. I was getting somewhere. The box to Dan was on its way. I exited the store, or so I thought. On my way, I saw the most wonderful nativity scene. If I were Christian, I would have purchased this for myself. Eldon! He would LOVE this. I had to have it. I pulled it off the shelf. Behind it was a statue of a girl, with both arms extended. On her arms were birds. It couldn't have been more perfect. I scooped up the items and took them to Mandy at the register.

"Can you wrap these for me so that I can ship them?" I asked.

"Yes, of course!" she replied.

We chatted about Bryce Canyon. She had grown up in Kodachrome and told me to go visit. I knew I did not have time but said I would. Back to the postal window.

"Well, hello, Sandy!" I said excitedly. "I bet you didn't think you would see me again so soon." Sandy cracked a warm smile. She was stuffing the slots above her head with the day's mail. "Did you grow up here?" I asked.

"Yes, in a little town called Tropic," she replied.

"Tell me about it," I asked her.

"It's not much more than some houses, a few restaurants, and shops." She was warming up to me.

"I figured I would come back and keep you busy. I have more things to ship," I told her.

"Oh, I am plenty busy," she replied with a quiet laugh.

"I know life has been a little crazy, but it's nice to laugh, isn't it?" I asked her.

"If you can't laugh at life, it'd be ugly," she replied. She finished preparing the package for Eldon.

I said, "Thank you, Sandy. It was sure nice to meet you!"

And with that, she put her right hand underneath the plexiglass. I know handshaking is a thing of the past, but I wanted to seal our connection. I took her hand in mine. It was the first stranger's hand I had held since March 12.

"Will you be back again?" she asked me.

"If you mean within the next five minutes? No, but someday soon. You can count on it," I replied.

"I'll be here," she assured me.

I booked a three-hour afternoon tour of Bryce Canyon with a local company, as I had done back in Jackson Hole. I met the tour group at a small gravel-filled parking lot. The owner told me I had been assigned to Timmy's bus. I grabbed my backpack and boarded the bus. Timmy was a seventy-five-year-old redneck with straggly white hair, dark sunglasses, hearing aids, and a bad limp. He was wearing a University of Florida Gator's baseball cap. I was sure I would get the UF story at some point. He asked for my name.

"Shari," I said.

"Sherry?" he questioned.

"No, Shari, like Shari Lewis," I said emphatically.

For the entirety of the tour, when he wasn't calling me sweetie or darlin', he called me Shari Lewis. I was not going to correct him. He could not hear me half the time anyway. He must have those hearing aids that the US government gives VFWs for free, like the ones my eighty-nine-year-old dad has. Dad cannot hear either.

Off we went to Bryce Canyon. Remember that science kit we had as kids, where you take handfuls of colored sand and squeeze it out through your tight fist and make castles? That is exactly what the hoodoos in Bryce Canyon look like. Just imagine the sand is all red and orange, with a little bit of gray on top. What a marvel! I thought Yellowstone and Zion were the most incredible land formations I had ever seen, but they were nothing compared to Bryce. I was in awe. Timmy pointed out different sand statues and told us they looked like alligators, crocodiles, Disney characters, mermaids, etc. He got to one that featured five vertical figures.

"Know what that one is called?" he asked. "It's called five cowboys in the shower, or as we like to say, *Brokeback Mountain*." At this point I knew there was a lot of political incorrectness headed my way. "Anyone from New York?" he asked.

"I am," I responded.

"Oh, then you might find this story offensive," he said.

"Timmy, you can't do much more to offend me at his point. What's the story?" I asked.

"Well, I had a busload of New Yorkers. I explained how the canyons were formed by water, ice, and gravity. There was this one guy who was busy on his cell phone and not paying attention. Once he was done with his call, he asked me to tell him how the Native Americans made the hoodoos. I thought, I am going to fix his wagon, so I told him that in the middle of the night, little Indian ladies come out with tiny tools and carve it all up into those shapes when the morons are asleep. The man had a stunned look on his face. A few minutes later, a lady pulled me aside and thanked me for putting that asshole in his place."

Oh . . . this was going to be a long three hours.

Most of us on the tour were over fifty. At one stop, Timmy said, "I know you old people have bladder problems, so let me know if you need to use the facilities."

The pièce de résistance was when he told me that he didn't realize he was a bigot until he moved to Florida.

It took a move to Florida to realize this? I knew it in about five minutes.

He was born in Georgia, moved to Miami, then to Cocoa Beach. He attended UF—hence the hat—and had moved from Gainesville to Utah. He had been there ever since, working as a guide. His final story was to tell us why we should not get out of the bus when we saw deer, especially a buck. "This one time I was driving a tour bus, and the vehicle in front of us had a load of Orientals in it."

WHAT? Did he just say Orientals?

"You know how those people are with their cameras? Well, about fifty of them got out of the bus, took out their cameras, and were taking pictures of a big buck. The buck got unhappy and started to charge at them. You've never seen so many Orientals run that quickly unless there was a big sale."

Oh my G-d! He did not just say that!

While we were driving back to the tour company parking lot, Timmy decided to share a few quips with us.

"Do you know why Utah has no crime?" he asked us. No one answered. "It's because everyone has guns here."

I thought back to Kurt and the evening holding the guns. So, the key to not having crime is to allow everyone to have weapons, making the neighbors afraid of being killed should they misstep? If the NRA had its way, every family would be armed and ready. This was concerning, but I kept my mouth shut. I was so dumbfounded that at the end of the tour I asked to take a picture with Timmy. I had to have proof that this man existed.

I handed the camera to another tour passenger. Timmy stood to my right. I had my arms apart, with one hand giving the thumbs-up sign. I waited in position for the man to get the right shot. Just as he went to take the picture, Timmy leaned in, put his arms around my waist, and his head on my shoulder. YUCK! I could not wait to get to my bed-and-breakfast to take a shower.

I drove twenty minutes to the tiny town of Panguitch. One flashing stoplight, a few motels, Panguitch House—my place for the night—several shuttered restaurants and stores, and not much else. Panguitch House was luxurious compared to Zions View Camping, and I would be grateful for the hot shower. The place was so charming and authentic. My name and keys were on a board when I entered the vestibule. There was a card to fill out, indicating my choice for breakfast. I completed it, put it back on the board, and went to my room.

I opened the door. I could immediately smell the caramel apple air freshener wafting throughout. It was adorable. Cute signs and sayings on the walls, a lovely king-sized bed, a full bathroom, and a shower I could not wait to enter. When I was finished bathing, I needed to find a place to eat. I drove around and saw nothing of interest, so I went inside the local market.

I grabbed a bag of salad, some cheese, beef jerky, yogurt, an apple, a banana, a bag of almonds, a bottle of salad dressing, a can of Arnold Palmer lite, and a bag of firewood with some fire-starter matches. I had noticed that the B&B had a firepit, and I planned to recreate my evenings in Zion. While at the register, I saw something that disturbed me, but I was intrigued. It was a Donald Trump talking pen. You could make the arms that sported red boxing gloves punch by pressing the back levers. Additionally, with each press, the pen spoke the following phrases:

Never forget 7/11.

I am the smartest guy I know.

Don't touch the hair.

I'm gonna build a wall.

Make America Great Again.

My IQ is huge.

Good people don't go into government.

You're fired!

I picked it up and asked the cashier, "Really? Is this necessary?"

"You would be surprised how many people buy this pen. We can't keep them in stock!" she said.

I CAN believe how many people buy that pen, and it makes me angry, sad, and disheartened to think that our election has come down to talking pens. So, I bought one.

I returned to Panguitch House, made myself dinner, and lit a lovely campfire. It was dark, quiet, and I was happily alone again. The clean, cool air was perfect. I sat outside until the fire burned out, put on my favorite pajamas, and tucked myself in. I slept for ten hours, and it was fabulous. I packed up my things and headed back to Salt Lake City.

When I arrived at the airport, I saw a woman, probably in her forties, playing with a tiny puppy. "What is her name?" I asked.

"Mabel," she said.

What a cute name for a dog.

"What kind?" I asked her.

"A micro golden doodle," she replied.

"What is your name, and why are you sitting on the floor?" I asked her.

"I'm Becky. I bought a ticket for myself and Mabel. I told the airline that Mabel is eight weeks old. When I got to the airport, I was told that a dog must be ten weeks to fly. So, I had to buy a new ticket and say that she was ten weeks and not eight weeks. The next flight leaves at 11:00 p.m.," she said.

It was only 5 p.m. She had to sit on the floor of the airport for another six hours.

"Do you have food and water?" I asked her.

She pointed to Mabel's doggie bowls—one with kibble and the other with water.

"I meant for you. Do you have any food?" I asked.

"No," she replied. "And I can't go anywhere to get some."

"Here," I said. "I bought these yesterday, and I can get more food at the gate."

I handed her my banana, the bag of almonds, and beef jerky, all unopened. Betsy offered me the warmest smile. I have always looked for ways to surprise and delight people, many times strangers. I was so glad I could help her. I know Becky will be a wonderful mom to Mabel somewhere in Connecticut. Seeing Mabel made me miss Benji, my shih tzu-bichon mix. Soon he and I would be reunited.

la la land

I had prepaid an inexpensive rental car and planned to meet my friend Wendy Hallin at a restaurant called Locanda Positano to commemorate our first meeting nineteen years before in Italy. Familiar with the phrase, "You get what you pay for?" I had innocently booked a bargain car that required me to take two shuttles to an obscure parking lot, alone and in the dark. Not happening. I asked Wendy to come and get me at terminal two. I would figure out what to do about the car later.

Wendy and I enjoyed a wonderful dinner al fresco and reminisced about our two decade–long friendship. I told her that I wished her uncle Garry (Marshall) was still alive to make my COVID journey into the next *Princess Diaries*. As I had found at all my other stops on this trip, it was so good to be in the company of an old friend. We toasted, ate, laughed, discussed her family drama, and talked about the future.

"I just want to get back on a cruise ship," she said.

I could relate. My last cruise had been back in February, and my sea legs were long packed away. Someday the cruise industry will be back, but when? In the meantime, I was going to continue my journey. Initially, I had been escaping. I had been looking for solace any place I could find it. But now I saw that I had been bringing comfort, joy, and friendship to others. I was no longer escaping. I was a voyager, and my disappearance act had become a meaningful journey. You know that saying, "It's not the destination. It's the journey"? I was living that mantra and embracing life as I had never done before.

The following morning, I called Michele Goulding. She had been checking in on me during my trip, and I wanted to give her some updates. It was not a good day. Michele was upset. After being stuck in the apartment in Chicago for months, she was finally getting out to visit a friend of hers in Asheville, NC. As Michele was walking out her front door, the phone rang. She told me that it was her friend in Asheville, who said, "Michele, don't come! I was out walking the dogs, and their leashes wrapped around my legs. The dogs ran, and I fell. I need to call an ambulance to take me to the hospital. I think I broke something."

I felt horrible for the friend and for Michele. Both had been really looking forward to their reunion.

"Meet me in Phoenix on Thursday," I said.

"What?" she replied. "I don't know if I can do that. I think I want to drive with my neighbors to New York and visit my mom just to get out of here."

"Michele, be spontaneous! Meet me. Fly from New York to Phoenix. We can pretend we are back on the kitchen floor in Camp Wenasco! It will be like old times. Get here, and I will plan a fun week," I pressed.

"You know what? That sounds like fun. I just might do it!" she said.

We got off the phone, and a short time thereafter, Michele sent me an itinerary on United Airlines. "Will this work?" she texted.

How could I know? I had not even bought MY ticket yet.

"Absolutely! I will pick you up, and we will have an adventure in Arizona, like Thelma and Louise, without driving off a cliff," I joked. We were set to connect in early October.

Back to the story. I woke up at 4:30 a.m. on Sunday, September 27. It was Kol Nidre, the service that begins Yom Kippur, the holiest day of the Jewish calendar. It is the day that we ask G-d to forgive us for our sins of the prior year. The Jewish year of 5780 sucked. If 5780 were pizza toppings, they would be dirt and worms! Not long into 5780, Michael had a massive heart attack, I had bunion surgery, and then COVID hit. It had not been going well since the 2019 Thanksgiving cruise on the RCCL *Navigator of the Seas*, when I took thirty-four family members to celebrate Aunt Helen and Uncle Shelly's fiftieth wedding anniversary. Yom Kippur would be a day to reflect, atone, and renew.

Jewish holidays always remind me of Gina (Valentine) Illes. Many years ago, I was in California during Passover. I asked Gina to celebrate with me on the beach. She had never been to a seder. We bought some wine, matzo, and dinner, sat on the sand, and celebrated like Israelis in the desert, with the bonus view of the Pacific Ocean.

This year, I would share with her a blend of Rosh Hashana and Yom Kippur, minus the fasting. Gina picked me up from my hotel in Costa Mesa, where I would be spending the next five nights, and we headed for the market.

"How do you feel about matzo ball soup?" I asked.

"Never had it," she said.

Great. Matzo ball soup, blintzes, and of course, challah. I picked up some pomegranate juice and a lovely bottle of California textbook cabernet. Pomegranate is significant in the Jewish tradition because it symbolizes fertility and love. I didn't feel fertile around Gina, but I certainly felt loved. Gina, George, and their younger daughter Eva, and I would say prayers together and enjoy a wonderful al fresco Kol Nidre meal.

Gina and I walked into her house and unpacked the grocery bags. Within moments, I had several pots boiling, a Vitamix blending, and four mixing bowls out to prepare the blintz filling and the challah dough. It got busy and hot in the kitchen. It was so much fun to share my traditional foods with Gina, especially teaching her to roll and braid a challah and stuff a blintz crepe. While everything was cooking, we reminisced about our times working in corporate America and our jobs in the incentive travel department in the late 1980s. It was challenging to convince corporate executives to take their sales teams to tall-inclusive resorts, where the sleeping rooms had no locks, televisions, or service. Gina was my supervisor but treated me like an equal and a friend. We had the most interesting experiences in a misogynistic environment when European men elicited behaviors that would later become fuel for the #metoo movement.

I have so many stories. In 1990, my boss, the six foot, five inch VP of sales, met me at my hotel room, on the way to a company dinner, entered my room, and pushed me down on the bed. I remember his face, inches from mine. I looked deeply into his large brown eyes and asked, "Do you think this is a good idea?" I waited nervously for him to make a move. Slowly, he lifted himself off me, and we went to dinner. We never spoke about it again. I thought he got the message that his behavior had been unwarranted. I was mistaken. Two years later, while in the back seat of a taxi on the way to a business appointment, he grabbed my hand and held it in his groin. It wasn't easy being a young woman in business. Just being a woman felt like a full-time job. Was this ever going to change?

In November 2017, I wrote a letter to my abuser.

I am writing to you because I need to get something off my chest. I have been watching all of these high-powered men topple off of their pedestals for months. They took advantage of young women and used their power in inappropriate ways. While I don't necessarily believe that past actions (those that were sadly tolerated twenty or thirty years ago) should be punished today, I do understand why women feel the need to speak out.

Although the men who harassed me were not celebrities, it doesn't make those actions any less inappropriate or impactful.

When I worked for you, I was a young girl, eager to have people like me. I was driven to be successful and climb my way up the ladder. I wanted you to think well of me, promote me, recognize my work. I was met with behaviors not unlike those experienced by some of these women who are now out telling their stories.

I remember going into the CEO's office one day. He asked me to shut the door and sit down. I thought he wanted to discuss business. Then he said "I really want to fuck you." I was speechless. I left his office and went to visit the director of human resources. She immediately went to speak with the CEO, but to no avail. He found it funny.

I remember being with you in a taxi on the way to visit a lighting company client, where you grabbed my hand and put it in your groin. When I tried to pull my hand away—you held it there. Eventually you let it go. I was scared.

I remember going to a sales meeting in Phoenix. You came to my room to pick me up for dinner. I was not ready, so I let you into the room. You pushed me onto the bed and got on top of me. I asked you if you thought this was a good idea? It didn't go further; you got off me, and we went to dinner. I was scared then too.

You are a tall, handsome, smart, and powerful man. I was enamored with you and at the same time afraid. Who would believe me or care? Would I lose my job? Would you no longer like me? I was young and naive. Maybe this was just business as usual?

I never told anyone about the things that happened because I used that job to move onto other things and have since found my own success. However, those experiences have shaped how I deal with men even today.

I don't know how many other stories are out there. I never asked. Some people tell the media. I think it is more cathartic to tell the perpetrator directly. You should know that what you did was not only unwelcome but frightening.

I have always had the utmost of respect for you. You are an industry giant. You are smart, charismatic, and one of the most incredible entrepreneurs I have ever met. I idolized you. I wanted to emulate you.

I am sure I am not alone and that harassment at this company was rampant. It's sadly just the way things were back then. I can only hope the world will be different for my twenty-one-year-old daughter who will be entering the workforce in June. She deserves better.

I got a call from the man's attorney. He asked if the details in my letter were accurate. I told him they were. He said he would speak with his client. A few days later, the lawyer called me and uttered these words:

"My client is sorry for his behavior and for making you feel unsafe. He wanted to call you directly, but I advised against it."

"And now what?" I asked the attorney.

"Do you have a lawyer?" he asked me.

"Do I need one?" I replied.

Something told me I did, so I retained a powerhouse female lawyer who specialized in sexual harassment cases. Of course, the statute of limitations prevented me from filing a lawsuit, but I was not opposed to ruffling some feathers and speaking my mind. It was something I couldn't do, and didn't do as a child. But I was going to do it now. I couldn't ask for money. That would be considered extortion.

My counsel contacted his.

"You are being offered $50,000, provided you commit to giving it away to a qualified charity. The other party wants a very air-tight confidentiality agreement and specified damages if you breach it," she told me. "And they want to pay me $10,000 for my time, which is nothing more than a bribe," she explained. "What do you want to do?" she asked me.

"$50,000 isn't enough to make him pay for his actions. I am happy to donate the money to my synagogue, but please go back and negotiate," I told her.

She did. And then it got evil. My former boss' lawyer pulled out an email that I had sent to his client a few months earlier, congratulating him on some travel award he had won. There I was, going back to my abuser. I continued to have this deep-rooted need to be liked.

The lawyer sent a scathing letter to my attorney rescinding the original offer, stating that I could not have possibly been damaged if I were able to write and send that one electronic message.

My lawyer was incensed and sent a strong letter in reply. Here is one paragraph from that correspondence:

> Ms. Wallack has suffered the fear and anxiety that young women suffer when an older boss engages in such foul and revolting behavior, imposing themselves on young subordinates as if they are objects there for no reason other than his pleasure and amusement. On account of these assaults, Ms. Wallack, like so many working women, was for years afraid to be alone with male bosses. She had flashbacks and deep anxiety that it was going to happen again.

Should I wonder anymore why I have anxiety and depression? Sure, I move on, but would it ever be possible to completely heal? No amount of baking could ever erase the past, but I continued to find ways to replace trauma with humor and yeast.

Gina and I have a favorite story involving a client named Frank. He was the ultimate chauvinistic pain in the ass. Nothing was good enough for him. No matter what we did, he complained. Each time we thought we were heroines saving the day, he knocked us down. I don't think he liked women. When his incentive program was over, we knew we had to write him a thank-you letter. How do you thank someone who has made several months of your life miserable? Gina pulled rank, and I wrote the letter. I do not have it anymore, but it likely said something like this:

> Dear Frank,
>
> It was our pleasure hosting your group. We sincerely hope that you and your colleagues had a wonderful time and enjoyed everything the resort had to offer. As you spent some time mastering the flying trapeze, perhaps you will consider staying with us again and perfecting your skills.

Please call on us if we can be of assistance with a future incentive trip. We would be delighted to host you again.

With gratitude,
Gina Valentine, Director of Corporate and Incentive Sales
Shari Rosenthal, Manager of Corporate and Incentive Sales

We looked at the very appropriate letter and decided that it would be fun to write what we really thought and not send it. That went something like this:

Dear Asshole,

Having you at our property was the worst experience of our lives. You suck. We hope you were miserable every moment. No one wants you to come back, EVER!

You spent so much time on the flying trapeze. Did you ever bother to entertain your invitees? You are the most self-centered person we have ever met.

It's a wonder anyone is married to you. How does your wife put up with your whining and complaining? It must get really old.

Promise us you will never come back. There is no amount of money in the world for us to want to put up with your attitude again.

With complete and total disgust,
Gina Valentine, Queen of Corporate and Incentive Sales
Shari Rosenthal, Empress of Corporate and Incentive Sales

This was before the days of email. Both letters were written with a word processor. Remember those? I printed both letters and put them on Gina's desk. I hope she mailed the correct one. Frank never answered.

Dinner was served. We sat outside. The weather was just perfect. Cool, clean, crisp air. No sign of the forest fires in the north. We lit candles, drank pomegranate juice and wine, ate melt-in-your-mouth matzo ball soup and challah. Everyone looked stuffed. I promised dessert would be worth it. I had made a coulis of rhubarb, raspberries, strawberries, and blackberries to put under the blintzes. I topped them off with sour cream and a sprinkle of sugar. HEAVEN. George asked if we could have them the next night for dessert. Fortunately, there were more waiting in the fridge.

After dinner, Gina, George, and I sat on the couch for a few hours until their cat's dander started to ignite my allergies.

It was so comfortable being with them. I didn't feel like a third wheel. I felt welcome and loved. Gina had known me in my most insecure and needy days. She remarked at how far I had come. She told me that she tells people, "Remember that girl who worked for me at Club Med? Well, you should see her now!" She has always been so supportive of me and happy with each award I have won, big deals I have negotiated, and figurative mountains I have climbed.

Gina is authentic, kind, warm, caring, and so funny. There is never a time we get together or talk on the phone that we do not laugh. She always has great perspective and has a very diplomatic way of advising me. She makes me think it is my idea.

Gina returned me to the Marriott Hotel. To say that there was a lack of services is an understatement. One employee running the property. No restaurant. No coffee. No small market to buy food. No daily maid services. It was like staying at home, but without a kitchen or washing machine. COVID had made this once-thriving hotel into a bed-and-breakfast, without the breakfast. Yet the bed was comfortable. There were a few creature comforts: air conditioning, Wi-Fi, and a huge flat-screen television. The first presidential debate would be tomorrow. I was all set!

On Tuesday, I slept in. It was the first time I had allowed myself to do that since July. I had planned to meet with some clients for lunch and then reconnect with Gina, George, Eva, and her boyfriend Malachai. The Marriott felt empty. The pool WAS empty. We could order in dinner via DoorDash, watch the debate, and then spend some time outside enjoying the hot tub and firepit. The phone rang. It was Jake.

"Mom, I have something to tell you," he said.

That was not a good sign.

Did something happen to Benji? Did my kid set the house on fire?
What could it be?

"Mom, did you send home a mug in the last box?" he asked.

"Yes," I replied.

"Well, it broke. Should I throw it out? Oh, and you sent some statue of a girl with birds on her arms? It's been decapitated."

WHAT?

"Well, I was able to glue the girl's head back on, but the mug is history," he said.

All I could hear was Rabbi Andrew's voice, "Shari, you can't go around stealing things. It will catch up to you!"

"Just throw it out," I said. I supposed I wasn't meant to have that mug. I wouldn't be stealing anything else on this trip. It's bad karma.

At 6:00 p.m., the debate started. I lasted a short time before turning off the set. It was more of a boxing match, with Trump and Biden talking over each other. "Will you just shut up, man?" Joe said. Looks like they will have to change the rules for the debates that follow. Maybe they can attach a wire collar that zaps one candidate in the neck when he interrupts or goes over the allotted two minutes?

We ordered in Asian food from Din Tai Fung, sat by the pool with a bottle of cabernet, ate, and laughed. The soup dumplings from the restaurant were delicious. I was sorry I hadn't discovered them until the end of my visit.

The service at the hotel had been less than stellar. The hot tub was out of order. Michael, the evening employee—I swear the hotel had only one employee at a time—could not figure out how to make the gas firepit work. But we had a private pool and patio to enjoy each other's company. It was awesome.

That evening I decided to firm up my plans for the next stop: Phoenix. I was going to stay there for three nights and then head to Sedona. This, however, was the first time that none of my friends were available upon my arrival. Sue had her granddaughter, Paisley, staying 'til Saturday. Linda and Dave were quarantining because their daughter-in-law had suspicious symptoms and was awaiting COVID results. Amber was tending to her mother, who had surgery, and the client I was going to visit had just booked a site visit to Las Vegas. Time to change course.

Perhaps I should throw Tucson into the mix. I had never been there, and it sounded exotic. I booked an Airbnb online. $100 to stay on a ranch in the middle of nowhere. Why not? I had been glamping in Zion. A ranch in Tucson would be the perfect encore to my outback adventure.

Gina stayed with me at the hotel overnight. We had not spent the night together since our twenties. We were like two middle schoolers escaping our parents. We laughed until it hurt. When we had worked together in the eighties, I was a very needy, insecure, twenty-something. Gina befriended me like the cool girl in high school who feels sorry for the dorky new kid and has lunch with her in the cafeteria when no one else will.

No one at work looked at me the way Gina did. She saw through my insecurities and deep desire to be loved at any cost. I remember wanting her approval so badly back then, and I am sure I did anything I could to get her attention and gain her approval. What I did not realize was that she always liked me for me, and I really didn't have to do anything.

As we sat on the bed, she turned to me and said, "You have grown so much. I am proud of you. It's really fun being with you, and I am so glad we had this time together."

I had finally arrived, I thought. I did not have to be anyone but myself, and it felt awesome! Before going to bed I checked my phone. During the past few months, I had given up my addiction to the iPhone and social media. After watching *The Social Dilemma* with Lynn in Park City, I realized the damaging effects of technology. I am as guilty as the next person, and I have been taking time to wean myself from the need to be continually connected.

I wished I had not seen the text message. It was from my friend Rhonda. We have been friends since our girls were in Torah school together at Ramat Shalom in Plantation.

Hi. I have some bad news. I haven't been feeling well for the past few months and just got the diagnosis. It's metastatic breast cancer. I have tumors on my lung and liver. Please don't call because it is hard for me to speak. One of the tumors is pressing on my lung, which makes breathing and speaking difficult. I am at University of Miami hospital for chemo and radiation. I should be here for at least a week. No visitors. I am not posting anything on social media, so please use your discretion in sharing this information.

Whoa! I immediately texted her and asked if there was anything I could do. I wanted to be there for her kids. I felt so sad. She had battled breast cancer in 2008 and fully recovered. This is a new cancer, she told me. I told her I would cook for her once I returned to Florida. She texted back: "Thank you. I have really enjoyed watching your Facebook cooking posts over the past few months."

I would bring her some joy, challah, and Jewish penicillin once I returned.

la la land

Gina spent all of September 29 with me. First, we met my friend Natalie Young. She was the cantor at Ramat Shalom when both of my kids were in Torah school there. With Rabbi Andrew, she officiated at my kids' *b n'ai mitzvot*. I was disappointed when Natalie and her family moved to Orange County several years back, but fortunately I have seen her a few times after she left.

We ate breakfast at Burnt Crumbs in Irvine. I shared snippets of my journey with Natalie, who immediately remarked, "You have a lightness about you. I am so happy to see you this way."

I told her that I had found a sense of inner peace and was thrilled to be on this journey. I shared that I didn't feel as if I belonged at home. She enlightened me with a passage from a Brené Brown book titled, *Braving the Wilderness*. I think Brené Brown is the Messiah!

Belonging is the innate human desire to be part of something larger than us. Because this yearning is so primal, we often try to acquire it by fitting in and by seeking approval, which are not only hollow substitutes for belonging, but often barriers to it. Because true belonging only happens when we present our authentic, imperfect selves to the world, our sense of belonging can never be greater than our level of self-acceptance.

Before COVID, I had felt that my belonging was as the president of Buy the Sea in the middle of the cruise industry. I feared that losing all or part of the company would mean I didn't belong anymore. I needed to realize this was far from the truth. I had to see myself differently. I had to remember that no matter what door could close, a window or two would open. I just wasn't sure of the view.

After breakfast with Natalie, I drove with Gina, and we ran some errands. Our first stop? A marijuana dispensary. They should just call it Adult Candy Store. With weed being legal in California, all you need is your driver's license and cash. Then you can buy whatever you want. Edibles! Why not? Surely these would come in handy during my trip. I bought a few containers of THC/CBD gummies and three prerolled cigarettes: cruise, calm and clarity. I'd be calmly cruising toward clarity at some point during the journey.

That evening, we cooked Pacific salmon, basmati rice, and salad. About the rice. Gina lived in Tehran as a child and has many Persian friends. She taught me how to make *tahdig*, which is easily made in a Persian rice cooker. You put rice, olive oil, and salt into this inexpensive, simple machine. During the final twenty minutes of cooking, the bottom layer of the rice becomes crispy. I love it so much I can eat an entire batch.

While we sat outside, Gina and George talked about retirement and what that would look like someday. Gina has been learning Hungarian so that she can apply for a Hungarian passport. Because George was born in Hungary, he is already a citizen. If the United States continues on its current path, perhaps moving to Europe isn't such a bad idea.

After dinner it was time to say goodbye to Gina. I didn't want to. It felt so good being around her. I had enjoyed our walk through memory lane, and I didn't want it to end. If she didn't have a cat, I might have just moved in! The thought bubble over Gina's head would read, "Good thing that old deaf cat is still alive!"

fearless

On October 1, I flew to Phoenix to connect with Michele. I was excited to have a friend along for the ride. We landed at Sky Harbor Airport and hopped on the shuttle to the Marriott Phoenix Airport hotel. In the morning, we took the transfer back to the terminal to pick up our rental car. The line to take the universal shuttle to the car rental lot was a few hundred people deep. We were stunned! What was even more shocking was that people were willing to stand outside in hundred-and-five-degree heat and WAIT to board a half-empty vehicle.

They can't be Jewish. No Jew would stand in that kind of a line.

I called an Uber, sped to the rental counter, and we were in our car in fifteen minutes. I am pretty sure those people are still in line.

Off to Tucson, a city of which I knew nothing. We drove down to Old Tucson, which was sadly closed. We decided to check out the San Xavier del Bac Mission. Several people suggested we visit it, the oldest intact European structure in Arizona. First, we would use the restroom, peruse the gift shop, and get a bite to eat. In the store, there was one baseball cap with a red cardinal prominently displayed. I had to have it. The specialties at the café were delicious: fry-dough tacos and the coyote float, a large root beer and ice-cream sensation for a whopping $2!

At 2:15 p.m., we walked to the church. We approached the door to the sanctuary. We were eager to see the Baroque architecture. NO! It's open only from 9:00 a.m. to 2:00 p.m. We had just missed it. We were so disappointed.

Off to the center of town. We passed the University of Arizona. I had no idea that the prime party school in America was tucked away in this adorable enclave. We decided to go window shopping.

I parked the car behind one with a custom license plate that had Arizona on top and cardinals on the bottom. Cardinals? Of course, cardinals! I later found out that the Cardinals are Arizona's pro football team. Now my jaunt to Tucson made more sense. We exited the car and crossed the street. A tattoo parlor. Yes! To get a tattoo was on my bucket list. I knocked on the door, and a young man came out.

"Can I help you?" he asked.

"Yes, I would like a tattoo," I told him.

We went inside, and he asked me to show him what I wanted and where I wanted it placed. I decided that it would be appropriate to put the sailboat part of the Buy the Sea logo on my ankle. The man copied the boat from my website and asked me to sit in a barber chair with my left leg up on a raised cushion.

"Ever had a tattoo before?" he asked.

"No," I stated. "Does it hurt?"

"That is all relative. It feels like a cat scratch," he replied.

Hmm. I could handle a cat scratch. Okay, let's do this! I clasped my hands tightly. He began to carve the logo into my leg. It felt as if he was dragging razor blades across my skin. It HURT, but I was going through with it. Now, no matter what happened to Buy the Sea, we would always be connected.

Off to our Airbnb. Ray Edwards was waiting for us at the ranch. His wife, Carol, was in Gainesville with her daughter, who had just had a baby. We punched in a code to get through the gates of Quail Oasis Ranch. As the iron bars opened, we entered nine acres of zen. As we drove up to the ranch house, we noticed a wipe board with our names on it. There were cactus plants everywhere, of all varieties, most prominent, the saguaro. That's the one that you see in every postcard of Tucson. It is native to the Sonoran Desert. I had seen them many times in Mexico when I went to Club Med Sonora Bay with some friends while in my twenties. When you get a blow-up of a cactus, that's the one. I imagined Wile E. Coyote and Roadrunner chasing me around Ray and Carol's sanctuary.

And of course, Michele started to describe the cacti in penis language. "Look at the erect one over there will the balls growing on top. Oh . . . and check that one out. The arm growing out of the side is totally switched on and ready for action."

Ray took us on a visit of his home. We were going to occupy one of the bedrooms with a fireplace and en-suite bathroom.

"The house is yours. Please make yourselves at home. Want to see the chicken coops?" he asked.

Sure. We went out in the back and met the hens and collected the freshly laid eggs. We told Ray that we were meeting a friend for dinner, but if he wanted to learn how to bake challah for his future guests, he would have to go to the market to buy the ingredients. From the fresh eggs, I would teach him to prepare cloud eggs. Ray went to the market while we showered. And then it occurred to me.

Was Ray an ax murderer who lured in unsuspecting women? Was Carol actually away with their daughter and the new baby? Was there really even a Carol? We were off the beaten path. No one would hear us scream! What was wrong with us? Anxiety central.

We left and went to dinner. When we returned, the house was dark. We entered through the front door. Ray was sitting in the living room.

That's it. He was waiting to rape and kill us. We were SO stupid.

"Hi, ladies," he said. "You are home so soon."

Was it too early to murder us?

I saw the ingredients for challah sitting on the counter. Okay, we would make bread before we meet our demise. Great. Trying to calm down, "So Ray, do you have a few bowls and measuring cups for me?" I asked.

He took everything out. I started to prepare the challah dough. All was calm. Ray was super nice and grateful to learn something new. He really was just a nice guy. He truly enjoyed having guests. He wasn't doing the Airbnb thing for the money. He wanted to share his beautiful home and sanctuary. Relief!

While the dough was rising, I disappeared into the leather recliner. I was exhausted. Michele stayed in the kitchen chatting with Ray. As I drifted off to a nice nap, I thought,

Wait, shouldn't Ray be afraid of us? What was wrong with HIM?

He invited perfect strangers into his home. There were no locks on the doors. What stopped us from waking up in the middle of the night, tying

Ray to a cactus, and robbing him blind or making him our sex slave or both? I decided to believe that there really are wonderful people in the world. I trusted the universe and my lucky star that we would be just fine in the morning.

I showed Ray how to roll and braid challah. He wanted a Plain Jane with poppyseeds. Before bed, Ray had two slices. A new addiction was born!

I woke up at 7:00 a.m. on Saturday. Michele had been up for hours because her inner time clock was on eastern daylight. As I exited the bedroom, I was startled to see Ray sitting in a chair just outside my door.

"Good morning," he whispered.

Oh my G-d, he WAS going to kill me.

"Cloud eggs! Let's make cloud eggs," I exclaimed with my nerves on high alert.

I would have a spatula in my hand at all times. We all know what a great weapon that is!

Ray went out to collect more chicken eggs. I escaped out the front door. I decided to walk the spiritual path that Ray and Carol had created on their property.

No one is murdered on a spiritual walk, are they?

I looked around. It was magical. Everything was quiet. The air was crisp. The sky was blue. And each inhale felt so cleansing. I sang a Carole King tune as if no one was listening. And thank goodness, no one was. King wrote that you have to wake up with a smile. If you show the love in your heart, people will treat you better. You will feel better. You will feel beautiful. Even with my gray roots, my chunkier-than-usual-body and my worn-out clothes, I did feel better. I felt beautiful on the inside.

Under the different varieties of plants and trees, Carol and Ray had written descriptions on terra-cotta pottery in black Sharpie marker. I learned that saguaro means gigantic candle, and these cactus trees can weigh up to six tons. Woodpeckers make openings in the sides of the plant to form a boot. Birds make their nests inside these entrances.

Saguaros live for hundreds of years. When one dies, the exterior dries and disintegrates, leaving a spectacular wood skeleton unlike anything I had seen before. I gawked at the Palo Verde—green-stick tree—which looks like something the Grinch would use for décor. The leaves, branches, and trunk are a stunning shade of green. At the end of the trail was a sign with a David

Steindl quote: "It is not happiness that makes us grateful. It's gratefulness that makes us happy."

The more gratitude that radiated from me during the past three months, the happier I became. And nothing in the world had changed. If anything, the state of the union had worsened since July 1. But I was better. Wayne Dyer once said, "If you change the way you look at things, the things you look at change." I had been putting good into the world and into myself. I had changed the way I looked at my connection to business and my identity. I had changed the way I viewed my adult children and my family relationships. I had changed the view and had taken back control of my life.

After a shower, I met Ray in the kitchen. He was eager to learn to make cloud eggs.

"I realize this is a bed-and-breakfast, Ray," I told him, "I bet you didn't know that we were the ones making the breakfast!"

Ray smiled. He was kind, gentle, and so in love with Carol. I had seen their wedding photo on the mantle. She was so pretty!

I jokingly said, "Ray, how in the world did you get Carol to marry you?"

He said, "I honestly have no idea. She is amazing. She wishes she were here to meet you. We have been doing this Airbnb thing for a few years, and I always say that Carol has one hundred new best friends. She falls in love with everyone who comes here and then wants to refund their money!"

I, too, was sorry I missed Carol. I could tell she was a special lady. Happily, I realized that Ray was kind, warm, charming, and best of all, he was not going to kill us! Staying at his house was a great decision.

After teaching Ray to make cloud "magic" and baking him another challah, it was time to drive to Phoenix. We were going to miss Ray and the short stay at the ranch, our Sonoran surprise. I hope Ray and Carol come and stay at my "ranch" in Plantation. Free of charge! Ray handed me my favorite trip souvenir, a dozen farm-fresh eggs to take with us to our next destination.

Michele and I drove the two hours to the home of Sue Hershkowitz-Coore, otherwise known as Speaker Sue. I had met Sue at least a dozen years before at an FICP (Financial and Insurance Conference Professionals' Association) conference. Sue's specialty is crafting excellent communication skills to help sell one's product. She is a grammar aficionado and has taught me that there are two very important parts to sending an attention-getting email. First, find a compelling subject line. Second, make sure you write the message with the reader in mind. No one cares about your needs. They want you to address theirs.

Sue and I became friends, and she has graciously mentored me several times throughout the years. Two somewhat hyper and driven Jewish girls from Long Island, working in a very gentile industry. It is no doubt why we clicked.

One of her best tips to me was to stop using "-ly" words, as they can be insulting and/or the delivery of bad news. "*Obviously,* you have no idea what I am talking about!" "*Apparently*, I am wasting my time explaining it to you." "*Unfortunately*, you will need another teacher." "*Finally!* You hear what I am saying." "*Evidently,* you are an idiot!"

When we arrived at Sue's adobe home in Scottsdale, we were shown to the upstairs casita/guesthouse. It was so charming, with its own terrace for watching the stars at night. Everything was perfectly chosen. The bedding, towels, and flooring were luxurious and welcoming. Sue had been watching my FB posts, and on one of them, she commented, "Can you mail me a challah?" I was going to do much better than that. I would make it with her.

Off to Safeway to collect the ingredients for bread and dinner. We bought Scottish salmon, wild rice—I had been hooked since my time in Minnesota—and salad ingredients. It was so relaxing just to sit in Sue's living room and chat. She is smitten by her three-year-old granddaughter Paisley. Sue's home office was overcome with Paisley's projects, and the living room sported a caged kiddie trampoline. I loved it!

Although Sue was amid a full kitchen renovation, we were able to bake challah and prepare dinner. We sat outside, and I told Sue about the book, *from hell to challah*.

"You need a tagline, Shari," she said.

"I do?" I replied.

"Yes, the people from McGraw Hill insisted I have one for my books," she added.

Okay, let's get a tagline. Michele, Sue, and I threw out some wine-induced titles until we came up with "from fragile to fearless, one grain at a time." It was cute, catchy, and explanatory.

We cleaned up from dinner and went to bed early. We wanted to be up by 7:00 a.m. to hike around Sue's house, which sat at the base of Lone Mountain. Of course! Lone Rock, Lone Shari, and now Lone Mountain. I'm in!

Let me start with, "I am NOT a hiker." I have neuropathy on my left side as a residual effect of back surgery in September 2012. The top of my left foot is hypersensitive. The bottom is numb. In January, I had bunion surgery on my right foot. I didn't have a pair of shorts with me, because I had mailed both pairs back home when I outgrew them. COVID-19, akin to the freshman fifteen, viral edition, was in full force on my five-four frame thanks to a steady diet of challah and blintzes.

At 7:30 a.m. the three of us were off on a "short" hike. We crossed the street to get to a huge park. I had to wear my Teva sandals since the fresh tattoo made the hiking boots painful. Not long into the hike, little pebbles infiltrated the sandals. I had to stop frequently to dump them out. It was hot. There were uphill stretches. I sucked water from my CamelBak 'til it was bone dry. We walked for what seemed like hours.

"Have we been hiking for four hours already?" I asked.

"Shari, it's only 8:30," Sue said. "We aren't even halfway done."

Oh. Shit! We'd only been gone an hour? I was not in any mood to hike another few hours. And I had to pee in the great outdoors. No shade. No privacy. I walked by a rock, dropped my stretch pants, squatted, and peed. I have come to realize that when you urinate while standing on very dry, hard ground, the liquid does not soak into the earth. It bounces off and splashes all over your legs and shoes. Awesome! I was now moist and partly naked from the bottom down.

I pulled up my pants and instantly backed up into a short cactus plant. Did you know that when the needles of a cactus hit your body, they detach from the plant and attach themselves to you? When you walk away from the cactus, the cactus comes with you. Ouch! One by one, I pulled the needles out of my thighs.

We continued to hike in the Arizona desert. There was no end in sight, and believe me, I was looking for one. When we finally made it back to Sue's house, I collapsed. No more hiking.

I am not the rugged outdoorsy type. I am a middle-aged, out-of-shape Jewish woman. Who was I kidding?

I prepared Ray's farm-fresh eggs, scrambled with cheddar cheese and truffle salt. Michele, Sue, and I enjoyed brunch on Sue's patio, which was getting hotter by the second. You know how they say, "It's a dry heat?" I don't care how dry. One hundred and five degrees is ridiculous, even without the humidity. You know that sensation you get when you heat your oven to three hundred and fifty degrees and then open it to insert something? Arizona!

We packed our bags and started the drive to Sedona. What unique activity could we do there? We had a brochure in the car that we had taken from the Thrifty counter.

"Hey, Michele?" I asked, with that zany look Lucy gets when she wants to convince Ethel to do something stupid. "How do you feel about a hot air balloon?"

"They go up crazy early, but I think I could be game for that," she said.

Before she could give it another thought, I had us booked for the morning of October 8. A hot air balloon ride was on my secondary bucket list, along with going bungee jumping in New Zealand and getting a tattoo. Since I had done both of those, the hot air balloon was certainly next.

Off on the Carefree Highway. What a perfect name for it. We were driving on the open road, headed for Red Rock paradise. You already know about my reckless driving in Beaver. Michele was being a good sport, although I made her a little nervous. She had a gentle way of correcting me.

If I was speeding, she would say in a soft, calm voice, "So you are going eighty, and the speed limit is sixty-five." When I was too close to the car in front of me, she said, "See how all of the cars have their brake lights on? You might be a little too close." If I needed to exit, she said, "You should start to think about getting in the right (or left) lane." Or my favorite, "You see the sign that says dip? That means we could bottom out the car if you don't slow down." I should have gotten the hint that my driving was intolerable based upon the number of times Michele said, "You know, I am happy to drive."

The first four times, I replied, "No thanks, I'm good." Upon the fifth suggestion, I replied, "So you said, Michele."

Michele is generally very relaxed. I suppose you need to be relaxed to allow me to drive.

If the roles were reversed, I would have been barking, "Hey, Mario Andretti, are you in a race?" Or "Do we need to be driving up the ass of the guy in front of us?" And "Get in the left lane already, dammit!" Or the always-appropriate "WHAT is wrong with you?"

We arrived at our hotel, Sedona Village Lodge, just outside the city. Picture a two-star Quality Inn. Okay, remove the word quality. How about Days Inn? You arrive and then figure out how many days you can handle being there since there are no services and no amenities.

Michele said, "It's fine. There is no riffraff around."

Exactly! Even the riffraff stayed somewhere nicer, but I was too cheap to pay for the Enchantment Resort, which would have been far too pampering for a gypsy like me! Truth is, we were happy to have two queen beds, a small fridge, a coffee maker, and a microwave. It would be great, and possibly a step up from glamping. There was one employee named Mitch on-site, like Stevie in *Schitt's Creek*. This one guy was the innkeeper, front-desk clerk, concierge, luggage handler, deliverer of towels and extra coffee, and resident expert on all things Sedona.

We dropped our bags and headed out to explore. The first thing we noticed is that Sedona has the only McDonald's with a green M. We were told it was quite an ordeal to allow a McDonald's in Sedona. The only way the city would permit it was if the company complied with the local rules stating that all buildings must be done with a color that reflects nature. I suppose green is more natural than yellow. But isn't the sun yellow?

We drove to Tlaquepaque, a Sedona landmark since 1970 that features over forty-five shops and galleries. Shopping was a good activity to do while the temperature was blazing. Once things cooled down, we headed for Little Horse Trail for a short hike. Thank goodness the tattoo was healing, so I could wear my hiking boots, which made walking so much more pleasant. Sedona is simply spectacular. Having seen the red rocks at Zion and Bryce, I was prepared for the sheer beauty and majesty found in this sacred and spiritual part of Arizona.

We drove to Whole Foods to stock our mini fridge with drinks, snacks, and ingredients to prepare basic meals. We didn't have the energy or desire to eat in restaurants three times a day. That night, for dinner, we had chicken apple sausages on farmhouse bread with a side of corn on the cob, sprinkled with the truffle salt I had been carrying from place to place. It was perfect. We were in bed by 8:00 p.m. Being a gypsy was exhausting!

October 5, we woke up at 6:00 a.m. After a cup of mediocre coffee, we headed out to find our first vortex. A vortex is a spot in nature where the earth is exceptionally alive with energy. It is a place where the earth's energy swirls and draws to its center everything that surrounds it like a tornado. At these magical sites, you will frequently see twisted tree trunks and limbs caused by the powerful energy at the core. We chose to experience Airport Mesa Vortex. I could feel the energy radiating as we approached and saw swirling sand close to the ground. I sat on a rock, played some meditation music on my iPhone, closed my eyes, and took it all in. It felt powerful and healing.

We then headed to Soldier Pass Trail for a hike. It was gorgeous. I was feeling one with nature. I sat on a rock and decided this was the perfect time to take out the cruise joint, which I had purchased in Costa Mesa, from my fanny pack. Calm and clarity would wait for another day. I wanted to completely heighten my senses and take in the beauty around me. I asked Michele to join me. A few hits, and we were sailing above the rocks without leaving the ground.

Michele and I can be silly without help, but this newly induced state made us giddy. Having not done this for a long time, I had forgotten what happens but was quickly reminded. You get thirsty, hungry, and start speaking gibberish, stating the obvious, and wondering about the absurd.

For Michele, it was the latter. "Look, the trees are green. Those cactus spikes look sharp. I think we should avoid touching those. The trail is fairly free of rocks. Do you think forest rangers come in the middle of the night to tidy things up for the hikers?" she questioned.

"Oh yeah, Michele, Yogi Bear hops onboard a sand-adapted Zamboni machine that goes through the entire area every evening!" I muttered.

Michele also has a habit of overexplaining everything to me, and at times, incessantly speaking. Picture a mom of three kids who has to constantly remind them of what to do and where to be. She was doing the same to me. This may not have been precisely what she said, but this is what my pothead heard: "Shari, let's look at the trail app. You did download it, didn't you? Oh, here are the options. We could go this way, which will lead us to this thing, and then we could turn and see that rock while making sure we don't hurt ourselves or fall. It would be horrible if we fall. We are all alone. There is no one here. I didn't bring a first aid kit. Did you put on sunscreen? Why aren't you wearing your CamelBak? You did fill it with water, didn't you? What if we run out of water? What if there's a fire? WHAT? You left the CamelBak in the car? What good is it going to do you in the car? So which trail did you want to do? Did you want to go left or right?"

I have absolutely no sense of direction. I can't read a map. Even with GPS, I get lost. Here we are in the middle of nowhere, and she wants ME to pick a trail? WHAT could be wrong with her?

We picked a direction and kept walking and walking and walking, most of it downhill, until paranoia started to kick in. Mine! We were lost. We would never find our way out. All I had on me was a small bottle of warm water, some almonds, and a stale granola bar. We were doomed. I started to panic. If we had gone the wrong way, I knew the hills were too steep for me to climb back up.

This is not the way I want to die, shriveled up from lack of fluids, and then eaten by a pack of javelinas.

"Michele! I know we are lost. We should have gone the other way. We are never getting out of here," I cried. "Call for someone to rescue us. I'm serious!"

"Relax. We'll figure it out," she tried to assure me.

"That is easy for you to say. You don't have a bad leg, back pain, and zero sense of direction!" I told her. "No one knows where we are!" I reminded her.

Michele walked ahead, and I followed, thinking this could be where I met my destiny. We hiked until we found the seven sacred pools, which helped me forget my panic and elder pain. The scenery was magnificent. And then I thought,

What if this is like the place where that mountaineer got stuck between two rocks, had to cut off his arm, and drink his own urine to survive? He had spoken at a conference I had attended, and I swore I would never go rock climbing.

We kept walking, which felt like forever. Just when I was completely out of energy and any semblance of common sense, we made one left turn and found the parking lot.

Shari, you are too old and too stupid to smoke pot on a desolate hiking trail. What is wrong with you? Seriously, what were you thinking? And what would the travel industry think if they knew that you get lost backing out of your own driveway? I know I am not adopted because my father and I share the same ability to get lost EVERYWHERE. Neither one of us can read a map either. At least I got his sense of humor. G-d divides.

I remember this time years ago when my mom took me, her little girl, shopping at Abraham and Strauss on Long Island. I was looking at pretty pajamas. I have always loved pajamas and have two drawers devoted to them in my house.

So here we were in this relatively small department store. My mom said, "Keep shopping. I am going to look at shoes. I will come back and get you." Dazzled by the sparkly nightgowns and soft fabrics, I didn't see which way my mom walked. I looked around for her. I walked to the shoe department, heart racing. My mom was gone. I was alone. She left me. I started to panic. Anxiety kicked in. I began to cry. I couldn't find her anywhere. Where was my mommy? Why did she do this to me? I was just a kid!

I sat down in tears. The security guard came over to see if I was okay. I told him that I couldn't find my mom. He sat down next to me. I calmed down. A few minutes later, my mom appeared. I ran to her and hugged her.

"Mom! Where were you? I was all alone, and I got lost in the store," I said through tears.

"Shari, I just went to the bathroom," she told me calmly. "And you are in college! You have got to be able to handle these things better!"

My mom, the security guard, and I laughed. The guard probably thought I had autism. I just suffer from a lack of a sense of direction and fear of abandonment. We'll have to save that for another time.

We drove back to the lodge to recharge and decided to visit the Chapel of the Holy Cross, a Christian church built in the shape of a cross in the 1950s. It had a serene, meditative quality and could be appreciated regardless of one's religious affiliation. Then we trekked a few miles of the Broken Arrow Trail. This was our most challenging hike, but somehow, I was able to climb up boulders, inside cracks and crevices, and along very rocky terrain. There must be something magically healing about Sedona because back in Florida it is a stretch for me to park a few rows over and walk into the Bed Bath and Beyond entrance at Sawgrass Mills.

At the end of the hike, Michele stopped me. "Shh! Do you hear that?" she said.

"Hear what?" I murmured.

"I hear animals. Over there," she said and pointed to the left.

All I saw was some barbed wire. And then I heard the rustling in the bushes. What kind of dangerous animals were in there? We didn't have a weapon, unless you consider my $29 hiking stick, the one I had purchased in Springdale, dangerous. Well, it did have a pointy tip. We stood and waited as a family of javelina walked across the path in front of us. Having never seen a javelina before, I didn't know whether to hide, run, play dead, or just stand there. Picture Pumba from *The Lion King*, but blacker and uglier. These were mean-looking wild boars. Did they eat people? I had no idea, and I wasn't going to make any noise by asking Siri for help.

Michele decided to videotape the event. I guess she was doing it in case we were found dead, mauled by these ferocious beasts, and all that would be left as evidence would be the video on her phone. The javelina passed by. I stayed calm and did what I could not to pass out. Once I got safely back into the car, I googled Javelina:

Javelina (tayassu tajacu), also known as collared peccary, are medium-sized animals that look similar to a wild boar. They have mainly short, coarse, salt-and-pepper-colored hair, short legs, and a pig-like nose. The hair around the neck/shoulder area is lighter in color, giving it the look of a collar. Javelina have long, sharp canine teeth, which protrude from the jaws about an inch.

I learned that javelina are herbivores. Gee, if I had known that I would have gotten closer and tried to pet one. Not! Enough hiking. I wanted to have a spiritual reading. It was the perfect location for it. I walked into a place called Crystal Magic and met Phaedra, who introduced herself to me and told me she was Wiccan. Oh no! Witchcraft. Okay, why not? She explained that she read tarot cards. All I had to do was ask her a question, something I wanted the answer to.

So, I said, "I want to know what happens when I go home. Will I be okay? What will happen with my business and my relationships?"

She dealt the cards facedown. "These cards are fated," she said. "That means these are your destiny. You cannot change them."

The first card was the hermit. "This represents your inner energy. You have gone within yourself to find out who you really are. You have been on a journey and are going to come out and shine your light and knowledge on the rest of the world. You will be a teacher, advisor, or mentor. The nine on the hermit means you are ending one path and beginning another," she continued. Then she turned over the sun card. "This represents an innocent child riding on a white horse. The sun is shining bright colors. Sunflowers signify success in business or career. You will be successful. This is the card of pure joy. Your inner child has been released and now you are feeling this inner joy," she said. Next, she revealed the death card.

I gasped.

"Don't worry. The death card does not mean physical death, but it does mean a major transformation that has already occurred or is still occurring. Death is an ending of the old to pave room for the new to take place. It is a major and necessary transformation and profound change. It is liberation. This is where you leave the past behind. Prepare for birth and renewal. The Death card appears when significant life changes happen. It is time to rid yourself of attitudes and situations you have outgrown that no longer serve you. Pave the way for a new stage. New things will come in for you if you let go of the things that do not serve you," she said. "This is another major arcana card, the hierophant. It represents your recent past, conventional wisdom, and spiritual growth. The number five on the card indicates changes, alterations, and disruptions. Let go of conventional wisdom and beliefs. You will become a person of wise council," she told me. "And then, the queen of cups card, which represents a woman who is in her element by the sea and near the water. This is an important part of your persona. Face the water, face your intuition and your psychic ability, which will be important in your spiritual growth. Queen of cups is also representative of someone who is nurturing, helpful, and compassionate."

The reading continued. More cards were revealed, and each made sense to me. Phaedra did not know anything about me when I arrived. I did not tell her anything other than I worked in travel and had been visiting various places around the country for three months. The rest was in the cards.

Feeling all mystic, it was time to go back to the Sedona Village Lodge and attempt to finish that one joint we started. You can imagine how little pot I smoke when one joint lasts five days! Next door to our hotel was a Chinese restaurant. We were told it was the best Chinese food in Sedona. Since we never saw another sign in town for this cuisine, we were convinced it was the ONLY Chinese food in Sedona. And Chinese food pairs well with marijuana, so why not?

We walked a few feet to the restaurant and were seated immediately. Our eyes were bigger than our stomachs, and we over-ordered. Sizzling rice soup, shrimp with lobster sauce, and mu shu pork. Michele was perplexed by the sizzling rice in the broth and started another round of incessant talking.

"Why does the rice sizzle like that? Why does it just float on the top of the soup? Is it actually rice? What kind of rice? Is it a special rice? How funny that it just sits there on top of the soup. You know the Chinese are big into rice."

"Yeah, Michele," I said. I just let her talk.

At one point, midsentence, she said, "I think I have lost my train of thought." My reply, "That is because your thoughts just left on the last bus!"

One little inhale thirty minutes earlier, and we were now high to the point where we had trouble filling the mu shu pancakes with the pork and vegetable mixture. As we ate them, the filling kept dropping out. Michele kept speaking. I have no idea what she was saying. I just tuned her out and continued eating and laughing.

The waitress was a chatty middle-aged Asian lady who kept coming over to talk to us through her windshield visor, no mask. She looked like a geisha welder. We decided that we should take the leftovers and put them in our mini fridge for our later evening hunger pangs. Why is it that after eating Chinese food, you are always hungry in an hour? Does MSG have some magic formula that makes you think you are starving sixty minutes after eating a huge dinner? No one I know eats a Passover meal and goes back in the fridge for seconds of matzo ball soup and brisket! Maybe Jewish food is heartier than Chinese food, or maybe it is some conspiracy theory that gets you to order extra kung pao chicken and house special lo mein!

By 8:00 p.m., we were in bed. There is not much to do in Sedona in the evening. It is dark by 6:00 p.m. COVID took away any kind of nightlife that had likely existed before. You can't go for a hike or a stroll around town. After a long day out, sleep seemed like our best option.

When I woke up at 6:00 a.m. on October 7, Michelle was already out of bed. We had planned to go visit a peace garden and stupa. I opened the bedroom door and saw Michele on the couch, enjoying a cup of coffee. Michele does NOT need coffee to start her morning chitchat.

"How do you sleep that long? I have been up since 4:00 a.m. Are you ready to go yet? Where is the stupa you want to visit? What else are we doing today? Did you want me to make you a sandwich? We have all this food. You want some turkey? You want some coffee? Seriously, are you getting dressed?

What are you wearing? Are you going to eat breakfast? Did you see my water bottle? Did I leave it in the car?"

I said, with all the kindness I could muster at 6:00 a.m., "Michele, sweetheart. Darling, please SHUT UP!"

Michele is a good sport, and she knows when she is overly chatty. I honestly didn't mind, but I was used to traveling solo, and it was interesting to be around someone who was speaking every thought in her head. The truth is, I was grateful to have her, and I could not have asked for an easier companion.

We headed out to the Amitabha Stupa and Peace Park. What is a stupa? Stupas are beacons of compassion that multiply and broadcast the power of prayer. At this stupa there were garlands of prayer messages and strings of small flags with powerful and positive thoughts. A large wooden Buddha sat near the center of a meditation site. There was a remembrance book the visitors could sign and offer their own prayer. Here is what I wrote:

I pray for strength and healing, for myself and for the world. Let's be kind, caring, and considerate of others and our environment. We need each other to get through this scary and challenging time. I pray my return to Florida will be met with joy and clarity.

Michele and I hiked around the site and found a medicine wheel, which is a circle of stones on the ground in the shape of a wheel with four spokes. There were instructions on a board adjacent to the formation. A couple was standing and reading the instructions.

The man said to the woman, "So we are supposed to walk this counterclockwise. If we walk clockwise, it represents death according to the Hopi Indians. How many times should we go around? Can you take my picture on your phone? I have a flip phone, and it doesn't take pictures."

She took out her phone, went to take a picture of the man, and said, "I can't get rid of the shade. Can you move? Keep moving because the shade is still there."

The man asked, "Do you mean shadow? It's YOUR shadow, and no, you can't get rid of it. So which way is east? Do you have a compass? Are Hopi directions different than normal directions?"

This went on for several minutes until the couple finally left. Michele and I went to look at the sign to make sure we didn't die from walking the medicine wheel in the wrong direction.

fearless

How to Walk the Medicine Wheel

Please always enter the Medicine Wheel at the east opening with a prayerful intent. The east represents springtime and sunrise. It embodies rebirth and the awakening of consciousness. Now travel CLOCKWISE to the south, which is summer, the noontime and the place of growth. This is the childhood phase represented by kindness and compassion. Now walk to the west, representing the fall season and sunset. This is a time of looking within, spiritual maturation, and right relations. Then continue to the north, midnight, which represents the elders. The north embodies wisdom and the spiritual renewal and cleansing of wintertime.

WHERE did this guy read that we were supposed to walk counterclockwise? Well, Michele and I walked the wheel clockwise, according to the instructions, and we were still alive. We found the couple a bit later, sitting at the most sacred meditation site on the property, chatting away as if they were on a first date at Starbucks. Maybe they both had dyslexia, since every sign around the area said, NO TALKING.

Since Michele wanted to do some more strenuous hiking than I could handle, I booked myself for four treatments at The Spa at Sedona. One-hour massage, facial, detoxifying foot bath, and a hydro colonic. Maybe you are familiar with the first three. The last one is quite interesting. It's a reverse precolonoscopy cleanse. Instead of drinking some intolerable liquid to empty out your intestines, this treatment involves a thin tube inserted into one's rectum. You lie down on a hard plastic lounge chair with your legs up. Your bottom sits on top of a sloped potty. Warm water is pumped through the tube into your intestines as you are filled up and cleansed. I know, it sounds horrible, but it's rather amazing. Robin, the technician, sat with me most of the time. That part was a bit strange and reminded me of my childhood. I would ask my mother to sit with me in the bathroom when I had a stomachache.

A hydro colonic lasts an hour. Between the toxins that came out of my body via the ionized foot bath, and the waste—mostly challah and matzo balls—that was removed during the colonic, I was now lighter and purified. My jeans still didn't fit, so I guess I will have to go on that no-carb diet when I get home, but this was a good head start!

Back in the hotel room, relaxing and eating odds and ends from the mini fridge, I made the mistake of turning on the vice-presidential debate. Wouldn't it be nice if the candidates answered the questions asked by the moderator? Did someone in the green room make Pence look even whiter than he is? They did a good job!

Moderator: "VP Pence, does climate change pose an existential threat?"

Pence's reply, "Senator Harris said that Joe Biden would raise taxes. President Trump is going to put jobs first."

What does that have to do with climate change? Can we please stick with a two-minute reply?

I was having a tough time watching.

Then Pence said to Kamala Harris, "You are entitled to your own opinion, but you are not entitled to your own facts." No one on either side should make up facts. And the fly! I know Ruth sent it. There is no other explanation. Pray for the United States of America, and for goodness' sake, just VOTE.

We went to bed early, to be up before sunrise. Michele woke up and asked me, "Are we wearing regular clothes today?"

I couldn't help myself. "No, Michele, we are going to wear those Fraulein Maria play clothes I made from the old curtains in our bedroom while you were sleeping!"

Regular clothes? We had leggings, jeans, and some shirts. How much more regular could we get?

We segued into Michele's, looking for her water bottle, which she swore I had stolen from her, and she accused me of drinking from her coffee cup. This was going to be a LONG day. Tom, our hot air balloon pilot, arrived, and with three other passengers in tow, we headed for the launch site. We watched as a small wicker basket was removed from the trailer. Were we ALL supposed to fit in that thing? The balloon was taken out of its casing and laid on the ground. A large fan was placed beside the opening, and the balloon was cold filled. Shortly, it levitated above the basket.

We climbed in and were given some basic instructions. Tom never said, "Don't jump or lean over the edge," which I guess was obvious. With a few turns of a lever, blasts of ignited propane shot into the dirigible. We were airborne. We were flying and gliding over hills, valleys, trees, and canyons. We could see the other balloons in the distance. It felt like a movie. I had to continually look down to remind myself of how high up we were. Tom was sweet and funny. I imagine he gets the question, "So, how many times have you done this?" quite often, so I asked.

He answered my query with a smirk, "This is my first day!"

He gave us information about the native plants and animals.

I asked, "What kind of animals do you see out here?"

"Elk, cows, and javelina mostly," Tom replied. Then he turned to me and asked, "What kind of animals do you see in New York City?"

"New Yorkers!" I exclaimed.

Tom explained the process of fabricating and maintaining a balloon and the certification process to become a pilot. Our small balloon was made in Spokane, Washington, for $68,000. All the balloons that fly for Northern Light Balloon Expeditions are made with green and yellow material, which Tom told us is the most durable. The baskets are made of wicker because that is the least expensive material and is relatively easy to repair. Each balloon has a different pattern, which allows the tracker—the guy on the ground in the van—to find you after you land. The more experienced the pilot, the more likely you will have a safe and gentle return. Tom brought us down without incident.

The only thing he said before landing was, "Bend your knees, and don't assume that hitting the ground means we have touched down for good."

We bounced up a few times before we finished the ride. After Tom rolled up the balloon and secured everything back on the trailer, we drove to a canyon for a champagne toast and a pastry.

According to hotairexpeditions.com, the tradition of a champagne toast after a hot air balloon ride dates back to the 1780s when hot air balloons first took flight.

The first manned hot air balloon flight took place on November 21st, 1783, in Paris, France, and was flown by Jean-François Pilâtre de Rozier, a French chemistry and physics teacher, and François Laurent d'Arlandes, a French marquis and soldier.

In the 18th century, hot air ballooning was a ground-breaking science. Because most had never heard of or seen a hot air balloon at the time, many onlookers were afraid of the "dragon-like" hot air balloons and would often attack balloons with pitchforks. Hot air balloons were also unpopular with farmers as they were not fond of balloons landing in their fields and disturbing their crops.

On one of the first successfully manned balloon flights, the passengers carried along a bottle of champagne to enjoy during the flight, but instead of actually drinking it, it was used as an offer of goodwill to the farmers whose field their balloon had landed in. The champagne convinced the farmers that the balloon was far from being a fierce dragon and acted as an apology or peace offering for disturbing the land and animals grazing in the field.

The champagne smoothed things over, and a tradition was born.

Today, upon landing, it remains a tradition with balloonists around the world to offer champagne to passengers after a hot air balloon ride and recite the Balloonist's Prayer.

We raised a glass and listened to Dale, one of the pilots of the other balloons:

"The winds have welcomed you with softness. The sun has blessed you with his warm hands. You have flown so well and so high that G-d has joined you in your laughter and set you gently back again into the loving arms of Mother Earth."

Tom dropped us back at the lodge, where we packed up our things and headed for Phoenix. No car ride would be as much fun without Michele. Her random thoughts keep me in stitches.

Me: Michele, don't you think it is weird that people here pronounce coyote like "kay-yoat" and make the "e" silent?

Michele: Well, you don't hear anyone say I am going to "votay" instead of vote, so maybe it IS pronounced "kay-yoat."

Me: Yeah, but in the roadrunner cartoon, Wile E. Coyote pronounces the "e."

Michele: Are you going to take lessons in pronunciation from Looney Tunes? From the same people who said, "I tawt I taw a putty tat"? Like, would you go to speech class if Elmer Fudd were the teacher?

Me: *Rabbit season. Duck season. Rabbit season. Duck season. Duck season. Gunshot!*

Michele: You know that movie with Susan Sarandon and Brad Pitt?

Me: What movie, Michele?

Michele: The one where the woman lives in a house and is pregnant and has a miscarriage?

Me: Nope, I don't know that movie.

Michele: Wait, wait. It was that one from Australia, not Susan Sarandon.

Me: You mean Nicole Kidman?

Michele: Yeah, her.

Me: What about the movie?

Michele: Well, it was filmed at my friend's house in Dairen, Connecticut, and they got paid all kinds of money. The filmmakers were able to make any changes they wanted to, provided they returned the house back to the original condition at the end.

But how do you put back wallpaper that you take down? I mean, how do they match it? I don't get it. Oh, and the neighbors on the cul de sac all got into a fight over who was paid how much money for the use of their driveways to park the trailers. I'll tell ya, it didn't end well.

Me: What was the name of the movie, Michele?

Michele: I have no idea. It's an old one.

Me: And why did you bring that up?

Michele: I don't know. I watch all kinds of weird movies on the airplane when I fly back and forth to Asia. Did you see the one about the queen, or maybe it was a duchess? She has this weird leg problem and is in bed. The actress won an Academy Award.

Me: Can you be a little more specific?

Michele: Yeah, the actress was in that Netflix series about England.

Me: *The Crown?*

Michele: Yeah, *The Crown*. Same actress. I think it's Helen Mirren.

Me: You mean *The Queen* with Helen Mirren?

Michele: No. That's not it. Wait, *The Favorite*!

Me: So, you mean Olivia Colman?

Michele: Yeah! That's right. And then there was this movie with that old lady and Donald Sutherland.

Me: Which old lady?

Michele: Jane Fonda.

Me: A movie with Jane Fonda and Donald Sutherland?

Michele: Yeah . . . it was this old couple in the 1970s, and they are both ill, and they take a trip down to Key West in their Winnebago. Wait, no, THIS is the Helen Mirren movie.

Me: You are making this up. I never heard of such a movie.

Michele: Oh yeah, Shari. It's called *The Leisure Seeker*. You've never seen it?

Me: No. Michele, I just googled it. It got 38 percent Rotten Tomatoes. There is the reason I have never seen it. I don't think anyone else did either, except for you.

Being with Michele is like being a contestant on a strange game show where it is impossible to guess the answers because the clues are so random. Imagine you are on the *$100,000 Pyramid*. The category? Things you would find in a kitchen. Michele's clues are your keys, the dog leash, yesterday's lunch, a candle, vitamins, and a television, instead of a refrigerator, stove, dishwasher, and utensils! You get the idea.

chapter fourteen

home sweet home

I t was Friday, October 9. Phaedra told me that nine is a powerful number for me. I was leaving the past behind and looking forward to life changes. I hadn't thought much about what would happen when I returned home. I was nervous and a bit anxious. I had changed, but what about the people I had left behind in Florida three months ago? Would they be the same? Did they morph as well? Would they be happy to see me, or would they harbor resentment that I had left? Would I be able to hold onto the joy I had been experiencing for three months?

One thing was certain; I needed to go back and shed the twenty pounds I had picked up during my journey. The last time I was this heavy, I was nine months pregnant. My new Rollerblades were waiting, and so was my future.

COVID was alive and spreading in Florida. The election was getting closer. The country was at odds. I wasn't looking forward to hibernation or hurricanes. I was thinking about entering my house. I remembered sitting in my bed, wanting to die on July 2. As much as I love sleeping in my own bed, would the environment trigger me? Would I go into my bathroom and imagine the armed police officers hovering over me?

What about Buy the Sea? Could I go to the office with the knowledge that we had lost even more business than when I departed? What will I say to

Caryn, Sandy, Jaci, Robbyanne, and Ana? I agreed to keep them on salary until the end of the year, hoping that COVID would be gone and business would be on its way to a full recovery. The cruise lines were still not sailing. Would our clients book future programs or continue to offer virtual events and merchandise rewards in lieu of travel? So much was unknown, and the unknown is scary, especially for someone with generalized anxiety disorder.

Breathe. Just breathe. You are a warrior. You can do this. You have grown. You are grounded. You have evolved, and you can sustain that change. It is all in your mind. You get to decide how the story plays out.

Michele and I drove to the airport. Like every morning, she was searching for her mask and a few other items that she was convinced she had lost. By now it was expected and comical.

There was a barrage of "See all of the cars with their brake lights on? Don't you think you need to get into the left lane? We need to find a gas station. Remember how horrible the car rental lines were when we arrived? This could be bad. We can't leave this car dirty. There is so much junk in here. Don't forget we need to top off the tank. Did you remember your sweatshirt? How are you going to get on the plane with three bags? What terminal are you in? Did you leave anything in the car?"

G-d, I love her! Michele is a great person and an even better friend. Before we parted ways, we talked each other through what would happen when we arrived back home. I told her that she would be fine packing up the apartment and listing it with a new real estate agent. I promised that if she chose to fly to Singapore before it sold, I would be stateside and would help her kids put the furniture in storage. She promised that if things got out of control in Florida, she would be just a phone call away. We assured each other: you can do this! It's going to be okay.

We arrived at security. I had Clear and TSA PreCheck. Michele had only a TSA PreCheck. We went in different lanes and were directed to the same X-ray line. There were two people, a woman and a man, between Michele and me. Michele was struggling a bit with her bag, so I walked ahead of the two passengers to join her. The thirty-something man became furious.

"Hey, what are you doing? Why are you cutting the line? I am in a rush. You don't have the right to go ahead of me!" he screamed.

"We are traveling together, sir," I replied.

"I don't care. You don't get to cut the line!" he shouted.

I wanted to stand my ground and delay him even further.

Maybe you should have timed this better so that one person in the line in front of you didn't make you miss your flight, asshole.

I gently asked him, "Would you like to go ahead of us?"

Now HE would be jumping the line since Michele was rightly in front of him.

"Yes, I would!" he shouted.

He shoved ahead of us with a nasty frown and miserable attitude. Not a thank you, which I didn't expect anyway.

As he grabbed his bag off the belt in a big huff and hurry, I said loudly, "That made a huge difference, didn't it? Have a blessed day."

Couldn't he have just kindly asked, "Ladies, I am in a bit of a hurry? Would you mind if I went ahead of you?" Who says no to that? I realized that for a good part of my life, I have wondered why people don't respond to situations the way I do. I mean, isn't there the Shari way and the wrong way? Just ask yourself, WWSD? What would Shari do? You may end up in jail with a tattoo and an incessant talker for a cellmate, but at least you'll have an adventure.

As Mr. Misery darted away, I remembered that life is 10 percent what happens to you and 90 percent how you deal with it. When people are that angry, it is about them and not you. I was not going to let some random jerk ruin my day—not today and not any day. The world is filled with angry, unfulfilled, sad, miserable people. It is also filled with kind, caring, loving, generous, and happy ones. My job is to avoid the former and embrace the latter. I can control only my behavior and my reactions. There are going to be more people like the angry dude at TSA. There is nothing I can do about that. The more I remember this, the better my life will be.

Michele escorted me to gate F3. My flight would be leaving an hour before hers. We took one last masked photo. If I had thought too much about saying goodbye, I would have cried. It could be years before I would see Michele again.

Maybe I could go to Singapore and teach the people how to bake challah? It's unlikely anyone there knows what challah is. Could be a new enterprise.

I walked to the jet bridge. Time to leave this path behind and look forward to the road ahead. I sat on the plane, leaving stop number eighteen.

As I sat on the runway, I pulled out my phone and went on eBay looking for something very specific, an orange coffee mug that said "Good Morning Sunshine." There was one available. I bought it, as I should have done in the first place.

The flight was uneventful, as all had been. Protocols were strictly followed, and I felt as safe as I could be. I listened to Trevor Noah's *Born a Crime*. I love that he narrates it, which makes it so much more special and authentic. What an amazing man! I see why he is so successful.

I disembarked the plane with my teal carry-on and black backpack and called an Uber. The twenty-minute drive back to Plantation felt longer than usual. We arrived. I got out of the sedan. I left my bags in the driveway. Usually, I wonder if the house will be clean, if the garbage was taken out, if the laundry was done. I wasn't thinking about any of that. I just wanted to see my boy. Did he miss me? Would he be angry that I left for so long?

I opened the door a crack. I heard footsteps. I stood and waited for him to appear and acknowledge me. There, with his big brown soulful eyes, was the one who wouldn't ask questions or reprimand me. He wouldn't notice that I gained twenty pounds or needed my hair cut and dyed. He looked up at me as if to say, "Hey, Momma, I am so happy you are home. Wanna cuddle?"

Oh, Benji, you are pure love.

With that, Jake appeared, gave me a big hug, and said, "Benji missed you."

I knew he was really saying, "Mom, I missed you." And I missed him more than he will ever know.

epilogue

What have I learned? Where do I go from here? Was this journey about baking, self-discovery, facing fears, embracing the strength of human connection, or letting go of the past? It was all those things. I realized that I had always had the power inside of me, like Dorothy, who could have clicked her heels early in the story and gone home to Auntie Em. I WAS strong, fearless, adventurous, powerful, capable, creative, and resilient. I just needed a reminder and an outlet.

We all have some challah inside of us, waiting to be baked. Your challah might be music, knitting, writing, sports, multimedia, learning a new language, gardening, sewing, or anything else that takes your mind away from your worries. For me, pushing through anxiety and depression was facilitated through cooking and sharing. The more creative and prolific I became, the calmer I felt. Challah was MY outlet. I transferred my energy into the bread and found peace and joy. Challah led me on a mission to visit eighteen different destinations. This is significant because eighteen is the Hebrew letter *chai*, which means life or living.

I have most certainly been living! I started this journey believing I would be going only to New York and New Jersey. I packed a small carry-on bag. Once I got on the road, I knew I had more to accomplish, so I traveled from New York and New Jersey to Boston, Charlotte, Pigeon Forge, Memphis, Mississippi, Chicago, Minneapolis, Tofte, Boise, Jackson Hole, Salt Lake City, Zion/Bryce, Costa Mesa, Phoenix, Tucson, and Sedona. Rabbi Andrew Jacobs would say there are no coincidences. I had not planned to stop at eighteen, nor was I counting along the way. Some things are *bashert*, which in Yiddish means destiny.

My journey is far from over. The country is still in the middle of a pandemic, the likes of which we have not seen since 1918 with the Spanish flu.

epilogue

I don't know what will happen to the travel industry. So many people are out of work and hurting. I do know that I am so very grateful for the eighteen years that I have stood at the helm of Buy the Sea. See any coincidence in that? I have had the privilege of working side by side with five smart, hard-working, and loyal ladies: Caryn, Sandy, Jaci, Ana, and Robbyanne. Their dedication has been exemplary in every way. Together, we have exceeded each goal and every hurdle set in front of us.

I am proud, and better yet, I am satisfied. That does not mean I don't have dreams or future endeavors. It means that for the first time, I am happy with what I have. Prior to 2020, my days consisted of chasing every sale, award, and accolade. I lived on Facebook. I wasn't being mindful. I wasn't grounded. Although I had happy moments, I wasn't truly happy. Happiness is not a destination. I have learned that happiness can be found only by looking inside myself and drawing on my inner strength. No one is responsible for my happiness but me. From now on, I am going to make sure every moment counts and is filled with friends, family, and meaningful interactions. I have enjoyed every single day of this journey and the privilege of sharing it with you.

And by the way, I did get the $400 credit from American Express for the security deposit at the bear house. I am also the proud owner of a Yellowstone nature chain, which I hope will help me remember to be calm and appreciate the great outdoors. The Good Morning Sunshine mug arrived and will join me for coffee every morning on my patio. Oh, and I am sorry to report that Gina's cat died. Sorry for her, but not for me. Her house just became hypoallergenic!

When I got home on October 9, the place was sparkling. Jake had taken care of every detail, had cleaned the house, had given Benji a haircut, had organized the drawers and closets, and put a cinnamon straw broom in the entrance, making it smell delicious. It was a lovely homecoming, and I was so very grateful.

My journey is far from over. The challenges for me now are to stay happy without feeling the need to run, lose the twenty pounds that I found on the road, and lead my team into the future as the virus continues to grip our nation.

In the meantime, I have memories that will last a lifetime and gratitude for those who welcomed me into their homes and hearts for ninety-five days. Each host received a personalized, handwritten greeting card from me, thanking them for their hospitality. I have said for years that social media, texting, and email have taken the place of one of the finest and oldest arts we have: the handwritten note. It is my intention to keep it alive.

Several people have told me that I was the last person they would have expected to have a mental breakdown. On the outside, I look as if I have my act together. I have two smart adult children, and my parents are both alive. I have love in my life. I own a business that has provided me with financial independence. I have many good friends and have traveled around the world. Essentially, my cover looks great. My book chronicles my inner drama that is filled with unresolved issues and conflicts. It is my goal to work through them and help others do the same. My hope is that this book will be eye-opening, cathartic, a platform for open discussion. Especially now, we need to hear and help each other as we continue to work through these challenging times.

One thing I know for sure; I love being on the open road without a specific agenda or timetable. During my trip I never purchased more than one airline ticket at a time. I always knew when it was time to move on to the next destination. With the help of Krista Jackson's friend Jeff, I have purchased a conversion van that Jeff is outfitting with everything I will need when I take to the highway again. I look forward to driving my new tiny home to the places I didn't get to visit in 2020. I have no doubt there are new adventures, people, and stories waiting for me.

The election is finally over. There are no more political ads! Oh, and remember that back pain I was experiencing during my journey? On November 4, I was taken by ambulance to Broward General Hospital, where I had surgery for a blown L4–L5 disc. The excitement never ends!

As I heal, I pray the world will too. May we all find our way to a healthier future.

For those who are suffering and in need of healing:

Mi shebeirach imoteinu
M'kor hab'rachah la'avoteinu
El na, r'fa na lah
El na, r'fa na lo

Amen.

epilogue

May the one who blessed our ancestors, Abraham, Isaac, Jacob, Sarah, Rebecca, Rachel and Leah, bless and heal those who are ill. May the Blessed Holy One be filled with compassion for their health to be restored and their strength to be revived. May G-d swiftly send them a complete renewal of body and spirit. And let us say, Amen.

additional favorite recipes

I love cookies. When I was a kid, my mother used to give my brothers and me four cookies, usually Oreos or Chips Ahoy, with a glass of whole milk before bed. If it wasn't cookies, it was one of the following: Twinkies, Devil Dogs, Ring Dings, Yodels, Yankee Doodles, Sunny Doodles, Funny Bones, Snowballs, Swiss Rolls, or Hostess Cupcakes. I should have had a big weight problem, but I never did.

My mother was not a baker, so I didn't know until I was older that I could bake cookies myself. I mean, I knew there were those slice and bake products, but I had no idea you could mix flour, sugar, and other ingredients and get fresh, hot cookies! Take this from someone whose mother made mashed potatoes from a box of dehydrated potato flakes! Idahoan. Hungry Jack. I liked them. What the heck did I know? This was from the same mother who thought a great dinner was fish sticks and SpaghettiOs. Imagine my surprise when my mother-in-law boiled and mashed actual potatoes in front of me. It was a glorious day!

Back to the cookies. Once I learned I could bake cookies from scratch, I followed a recipe for chocolate chip cookies. I didn't like them. They tasted salty and sour. Everyone else said how delicious they were.

Maybe I only like Chips Ahoy? Maybe home-baked goods weren't my thing?

I decided to try again and went back to the store to buy more chocolate chips. They didn't have any more of the semisweet variety, so I bought milk chocolate chips. BINGO! I LOVE chocolate chip cookies. I just don't like semisweet chocolate. So here is the best chocolate chip cookie recipe you will ever find.

your last chocolate chip cookie recipe

3 cups flour

1 cup white, granulated sugar

1 cup light brown sugar

1 tsp sea salt

1 tsp baking soda

½ tsp baking powder

1 cup sweet butter (softened)

1 12-oz bag of milk chocolate chips

2 tsp vanilla

2 eggs

1 healthy handful of minced pecans (if desired)

Preheat oven to 375 degrees. Put parchment paper on a large baking sheet.

Cream together the sugars and butter with a hand or stand mixer. Once creamy, add in one egg at a time and then the vanilla.

In a separate bowl, combine the powdered ingredients. Slowly add those ingredients into the bowl with the sugar mixture. Mix until blended. Stir in the chocolate chips and nuts.

This recipe will make thirty-six large cookies. I make fifty smaller ones. Take healthy teaspoonful scoops of cookie dough and form balls. Place them on the cookie sheet far apart as the dough will spread.

The recipe says to bake for eight to ten minutes and remove from the oven when the cookies turn light brown. I like a very crispy cookie, so I leave them in the oven for twelve minutes. Less cooking time yields chewier cookies. Get crazy. Add chopped dried cherries!

My grandmother was a great cook. Our entire family would rave about her coleslaw. Her secret was her ability to shave down the cabbage as thin as possible. We never had a family barbecue or Thanksgiving without Grammy Esther's coleslaw. My mother and I have tried to replicate it, but we are always in too much of a hurry. It's delicious, and better than any deli!

grammy esther's coleslaw

1 head of shredded cabbage

1 cup of shredded carrots

1 shredded green pepper

salt and pepper to taste

celery salt

½ cup of vinegar

½ cup sugar

½ cup mayonnaise

Slice vegetables as thin as possible.

Add vinegar and sugar mixture.

Mix and then add the carrots and pepper.

Add mayo, salt, pepper, and celery salt.

Refrigerate overnight for best taste.

When I got married, my mother-in-law, Enid Wallack, gave me a cookbook that was a compilation of recipes from dozens of Hadassah members in Rochester, New York. My favorite one is Passover-friendly sweet and sour meatballs. Light, fluffy, and delicious! You don't have to be Jewish, and it doesn't have to be Passover for you to enjoy these! Great as an appetizer or main course.

rochester hadassah sweet and sour meatballs

2 pounds ground beef

1 large onion, diced

½ cup matzo meal

½ cup lemon juice

2 eggs, slightly beaten

1 cup sugar

½ cup minced onion

1 11-oz can tomato sauce

1 tsp salt

½ cup water

¼ tsp pepper

Combine beef, matzo meal, water, eggs, minced onion, salt, and pepper. Shape into meatballs. In a large pot, put the remaining ingredients and bring to a boil. Add meatballs, reduce heat, and simmer for one hour. Makes six servings.

I studied French in high school and college. As a young adult, I was on an international cooking kick. I made my family eat flan and paella for an entire month when I was trying out Spanish cuisine. We never ate flan again! I was always fascinated with French cuisine. I was into cream puffs once, which was not as crazy as my veal with mushrooms and cream sauce obsession. No one in my family wants to see veal ever again! I moved on to short ribs, which are insanely delicious!

short ribs niçoise

5 lbs short ribs

diced onion

head of celery, cleaned and sliced

10 carrots, peeled and sliced

head of garlic, minced

2 large cans of chopped tomatoes

jar of pitted kalamata olives, drained

box of beef or vegetable broth

bottle of red wine—must be drinkable

herbes de Provence

olive oil

salt and pepper

Rub the short ribs with salt and pepper. Put some olive oil in a large, heavy pot that has a lid. The heavier the better.

Sear short ribs in olive oil so that all sides are browned. Remove from the pot. Add in minced garlic, onion, and herbes de Provence. Cook until onions are translucent (a few minutes). Add back in the short ribs and all other ingredients. If there is not enough liquid, add another box of broth. Cook over low heat for three hours. Before serving, skim fat off the liquid.

I had never liked cooked salmon. Smoked and raw salmon are delicious, but the cooked version always tasted awful. That is because I kept trying farmed Atlantic salmon. When I discovered Scottish, Alaskan, Norwegian, and Faroe Islands salmon, my opinion completely changed. This is my favorite way to enjoy it!

---

sweet wild salmon

1 lb filet of Scottish or Alaskan salmon, skin on

brown sugar

whole-grain mustard

soy sauce

Mix the sugar, mustard, and soy sauce together to form a paste. Spread over the fish and bake for thirty minutes at 350 degrees. If your fish is very thin, reduce cooking time to twenty minutes.

My mother did all the cooking when I was a kid. My father knew how to make a few things: loosely scrambled eggs, crispy bacon, anything that can be cooked on a barbecue, and Daddy's Special Sauce. Seriously, this is what we called it. My brothers and I loved it. For years, Dad wouldn't tell us what was in it. When I was in college, he finally gave me the recipe. I thought this was a perfectly normal dish to make for dinner. I used to get excited on the nights Dad would prepare this delicacy. When I told my friends about it, they were horrified that any parent would feed this to their kids. I survived, happily.

daddy's special sauce

Heinz ketchup

unsalted butter

Kraft parmesan cheese (the kind that you don't need to refrigerate).
No comment! And yeah, I still like it! I know it's weird, but it's home!
Now I use real cheese. I have come up in the world.

Boil a box of spaghetti.

Drain the spaghetti.

In a small saucepan, put in equal amounts of ketchup and butter
and heat until the butter melts. Pour over spaghetti. Add cheese if
desired.

I know what it sounds like. My kids won't touch it. Every now and then
I make it. It's comfort food. Don't judge me. One update to Dad's recipe. I
use real parmesan cheese!

Following the tragic events that took place on February 14, 2018, in Parkland, Florida, a group of talented artists produced a concert called "From
Broadway with Love." Since the event venue is a few miles from my home,
I volunteered to house the production team, run errands, deliver food to
the artists, and be on call to assist where needed. Performers were being
flown in, mostly from New York, and some were going to arrive late in the
evening. They would be hungry, and nothing would be open late at night. I
made sandwiches and delivered them to the hotels. I call this sandwich the
Christy Altomare. Christy played Anastasia in the Broadway musical for its
entire run. She was so smitten with this compilation that I named it for her.

the christy altomare sandwich

ciabatta bread or any bread with a crunchy crust

Brie or Camembert cheese with the rind removed

arugula

red raspberry jam

thinly sliced turkey

thinly sliced Granny Smith apple

Cut a piece of bread from the loaf and then cut it in half. Spread raspberry jam on one side and softened cheese on the other. Layer the apple on one half and turkey on the other half. Then put arugula on either side. Connect the two halves. Enjoy! If you don't like raspberry, choose another flavor. Make sure you use jam and not jelly.

My cousins in North Carolina celebrate Christmas in a big way. One of their traditions is baking and decorating cookies. My cousin Casey's favorite is the eggnog cookie. I love cookies, and I really enjoy eggnog during the holidays, especially in my coffee.

melissa's holiday eggnog cookies

¾ cup sugar

¾ cup butter, softened

⅓ cup eggnog

1 egg

1 tsp baking powder

½ tsp nutmeg

¼ tsp salt

1 tsp vanilla

2 ½ cups flour

Combine sugar and butter. Beat until creamy. Add in eggnog, egg, and vanilla. Continue beating until combined. Sift remaining ingredients and then add to the creamy mixture. Blend.

Refrigerate the dough for at least one hour. Remove from the refrigerator and place on a floured board or countertop. Roll out the dough to the desired thickness and use a cookie cutter to make various shapes. You can add sprinkles before baking, or you can glaze or frost after the cookies are baked and fully cooled.

Bake in a 375 degree oven for eight to ten minutes, longer if the cookies are very thick. These cookies do not spread or rise much when baking, so you don't need to space them far apart on the cookie sheet. Use parchment paper, and cookies won't stick to the pan.

alexandra's truffled potatoes

1 bag of thin-skinned white or red potatoes

lemon juice

truffle salt

olive oil

herbes de provence

rosemary—fresh or dried

additional favorite recipes

Just say truffle, and I will come running. I love the smell and taste. I put truffle salt on almost everything. I discovered truffle dust while in Jackson Hole. It is sheer heaven—Jackson Hole AND the truffle dust. I put it on cloud eggs, meat, fish, vegetables, pasta, rice, and just about anything. If there were truffle ice cream, I would surely eat it! I made these truffled potatoes for Alexandra when she and Etai visited. They are now her favorite, and Etai's too.

Slice or quarter small white or red potatoes. In a bowl, toss them with lemon juice, olive oil, herbes de Provence, rosemary, and either truffle powder or truffle salt. If you use the dust, you may want to add some table salt.

Spread the potatoes in a single layer on a cookie sheet. I put a piece of aluminum foil on the bottom to make cleanup easier.

Cook in a 375 degree oven until the potatoes are soft on the inside and browned on the outside. I can't tell you how long without knowing how thick the chunks are, but at least thirty minutes.

Enjoy hot out of the oven. I won't judge you if you dip in ketchup. Just make sure it's Heinz!

acknowledgments

Minerva Morris—for being the best book editor, sidekick, armchair therapist, lunch mate, coffee date, and enthusiastic consumer of everything I have been cooking and baking along the way. I don't know which one of us had more fun working on this memoir. I am delighted that you love the story as much as I do. I am so grateful to you for inspiring me. You were an exceptional teacher for my children, but I feel that I got the best education of all. Thank you for being my cheerleader. I adore you!

Caryn—THANK YOU for sending me to time-out. I am grateful that you cared enough to protect me from myself. You did the right thing and I am so sorry that I scared you. Thanks for cheering me on. I know it's hasn't been easy being wrapped up in the Shari tornado for twenty-five years, and I thank you for being by my side, talking me off the ledge, letting me win at Scrabble, and loving me just the way I am. You are the best partner, side kick and soul mate a girl could have. ITACLY.

Lindsay—for putting your RISD degree to exceptional use and designing the perfect book cover art. You hold a special place in my heart.

Dad—for teaching me to how to fish, to handicap horses, to never split tens, and to negotiate any deal. Without that sense of humor you gifted me I could have never written this memoir. Happy 90th birthday!

Dr. Helene Cohen—for listening without judgment and validating me.

Esther Strassner of blessed memory—for her delicious blintzes.

Etai—for encouraging me to spend some time with Shari. I didn't realize how much I needed it!

Herman Rosenthal of blessed memory—for his floating matzo balls.

Jay—for being the only other person in my life who can understand my childhood and help me process my feelings and disappointments. Thanks for always being a phone call away. You are the best brother a girl could ask for. I'm sorry I pulled your hair! I love you.

acknowledgments

Mark Fretz—the first person to call me intrepid. If the shoe fits . . . I sincerely appreciate you!

Evan Phail—for your patience and partnership through the publishing process. I couldn't have done this without you!

Hannah Temel, a survivor of Nazi atrocities, and someone who has experienced real pain, loss, and despair. You are the strongest, most positive person I know. I am so grateful to have you in my life. You are a roadmap for positivity, goodness, and light. Thank you for your words of wisdom and encouragement always.

Michael—for helping me bring two strong, smart, and creative humans into the world. Thanks for your support and for continuing to be the president of the Shari Wallack fan club. Maybe one day there will be more than one member!

Kevin McCollum—for pushing me to dig deep, be vulnerable, and embrace little Shari. You are a treasure. Let's find a Broadway home for this crazy ride! A girl can dream.

Mom—for letting me share your secret sauce. You taught me about unconditional love. Thank you for always making me feel safe, for racing to my side, and for believing in me always. You taught me how to share everything with everyone. I love you to the moon and back.

Rabbi Andrew Jacobs—for reminding me that there are no coincidences and encouraging me to be more than just Jew "ish."

Jane Reilly—the most incredible publicist and now friend. Your enthusiasm and encouragement are astounding. You make me feel like the most accomplished author and baker! I am so lucky to have you in my life. Let's go sailing soon! You are a rock star.

David Quinn, my magical unicorn—thanks for your invaluable advice, mentorship, honesty, and love. You encouraged me to strengthen the story and create the most appropriate and clever cover. I am so grateful for you.

Rhonda Rotstein – you are always in my heart. Fuck cancer.

The fierce five ladies at Buy the Sea—for understanding that I had to go. Thanks for holding down the fort and believing in me. You are the wind beneath my wings.

Carole King—your songs got me through my childhood. They also get me through my adulthood. "You're beautiful as you feel."

acknowledgments

Special acknowledgments to the friends and family who counseled me, agreed to host me, cooked with me, entertained me, and played supporting roles in this story:

Adam Goldstein
Alexandra Socha
Amber Streeper
Blue Family
Bobbi and Mike Landreth
Cantor Natalie Young
Caroline Nussbaum
Casey, Melissa, Leah, Logan, Livvy, Luke, and Adalie Strassner
Celeste Bernardo
Dan and Silva Young
Eldon, Tricia, Maxwell, Jackson, Claire, and Annie Gale
Francisco Robleto, Jr.
Gaudreau family
Gina and George Illes
Helen Kerper
Inessa Illes
Jon Cryer
Judy and Jeff Locketz
Kerry Sanders
Koleen Roach
Krista, Kurt, and Layne Jackson
Michele Goulding
Michelle Fee
Orville and Heidi Thompson
Pat Miller
Rabbi Andrew Jacobs
Randall Phillips
Phil Rosenthal
Robyn Kaiyal
Roy Lewis
Ruth Levine Schmid
Sue Hershkowitz-Coore

acknowledgments

Sydney Steele
Teva Benshlomo
Vicki Freed
Wendy Hallin
Wendy Liebman
Yoni Benshlomo